Also by Moshe Lewin

Political Undercurrents in Soviet Economic Debates: From Bukharin to the Modern Reformers

Lenin's Last Struggle

Russian Peasants and Soviet Power: A Study of Collectivization

The Making of the Soviet System: Essays in the Social History of Interwar Russia

The Gorbachev
Phenomenon

The Gorbachev Phenomenon

A Historical Interpretation

Expanded Edition

Moshe Lewin

UNIVERSITY OF CALIFORNIA PRESS

BERKELEY · LOS ANGELES

Expanded Edition published 1991 by

University of California Press
Berkeley and Los Angeles, California

©1988, 1991 by
The Regents of the University of California

Library of Congress Cataloging-in-Publication Data

Lewin, Moshe, 1921–
    The Gorbachev phenomenon : a historical inter-
pretation / Moshe Lewin. — Expanded ed.
        p.   cm.
    Includes bibliographical references and index.
    ISBN 0-520-07429-7 (pbk.)
    1. Soviet Union—History—1953–   2. Gorbachev,
Mikhail Sergeevich, 1931–   . 3. Perestroïka. I. Title.
DK286.L48   1991
947.085—dc20   90-46995
                                                                    CIP

Printed in the United States of America

08   07   06   05   04
9   8   7   6

The paper used in this publication meets the minimum
requirements of ANSI/ NISO Z39.48-1992 (R 1997)
(*Permanence of Paper*). ∞

Contents

Preface   vii

Introduction   1

PART ONE *From Village to Megacity—*
             A Country in a Hurry

  1. The Rural Dimension, from the Tsars to Stalin   13
  2. The Rise of the Cities   30
  3. Urban Society, a New Labor Force   43
  4. The Intelligentsia   57
  5. The Urban Microworlds and Their Power   63
  6. Underpinnings of Public Opinion   72

PART TWO *The New Course*

  7. The Social Sciences: A New Ideology   85
  8. "Planned Imbalances," the Making of a Crisis   101
  9. The Way Out: A New Line   112
10. Gorbachev's Challenge   122
11. The Political Program: A One-Party Democracy?   129
12. The Economic Hurdle: Planning and Markets   136
    Conclusion   145

PART THREE *The End of the Gorbachev*
               Phenomenon?

13. Perestroika: The Genie Out of the Bottle   157
14. In Search of Clues in the Past   175

    Bibliography   187

    Index   195

Preface

The manuscript of this book was completed in February 1987. Naturally, events in the Soviet Union have continued to unfold, and phenomena barely visible in early 1987 are by now routinely covered in the world press.

But historians are not in the business of chasing after each day's events, a domain rightly reserved for journalists and commentators. Nonetheless, current events need not be off-limits to scholars. There is a genre, attempted in this book, that can be called "the history of the present." What distinguishes such an account from a mere inventory of episodes and incidents—what makes it history—is that the events are observed as belonging to a process, a continuity that has some direction, passes through stages, and crosses some thresholds.

Precisely this concept of a historical stage is the key to my arguments and assessments. By surveying the longer stretch of Russian and Soviet social history, I have tried to put recent events in some context. For the study of Russian/Soviet social classes, demographics, culture, economics, and politics enables us to see that each time the parameters of the social system have changed, a new phase was reached in the country's development. Of course, the appearance of a new historical stage is never reflected equally in all areas of life. Whenever some aspects of the system seriously lag behind others—for example, if the political institutions are too sluggish—crisis and turmoil, reform or stagnation, if not worse, invariably ensue. This is the story of the Soviet Union in the twentieth century.

Many Western analysts, however, have ignored the vast changes in the Soviet social system (urbanization, industrialization, the growth of the professional and intellectual classes) and diagnosed only stagnation and decline. This misguided orientation has led them to oversimplify a very complicated picture and to misinterpret precipitous transformations that have taken place in the USSR in the last half century. The reforms attempted by Nikita S. Khrushchev, and later by Aleksei N. Kosygin, for example, were dismissed in the West as merely another fit of ineffectual reformist hankerings that inevitably left the Soviet system ever the same.

In real life, though, nothing is really ever the same. To observers attuned to the dynamics of the Soviet historical process, the proposed economic reforms of the 1960s and their obvious failure were a sign of things to come. As I have argued elsewhere (*Political Undercurrents in Soviet Economic Debates: From Bukharin to the Modern Reformers*, Princeton, 1974), these events confirmed a new era in the making: the emerging phenomenon of a "civil society recovering" heralded the softening of Soviet statism, a modulation that would eventually produce serious mutations throughout the entire system. The nation's poor economic performance and accumulating inefficiencies were deeply affecting society and culture, but efforts to change the economic model were blocked by the political model, which was incapable of activating the nation's social and cultural reserves.

The neglected and misunderstood interconnection of the system's basic spheres—the relationship between economics and politics, for example—was to become the hub of the Soviet predicament. But in the 1960s politicians and reformers were only beginning, and very timidly at that, to analyze the problem in these terms. Conditions were not yet ripe for would-be reformers to realize the full complexity and scale of reforms that would have to be undertaken. The economy was still viewed as the only autonomous sphere; with the Soviet social structure being so poorly understood, people, especially among the political elite, were slow to appreciate the autonomy and relevance of the cultural sphere. The country's elites were not yet ready, politically and intellectually, to work out an adequately encompassing analysis and the needed grand-scale reforms.

Today, however, the Soviet leadership both understands the call of the times and possesses the political courage and intellectual wherewithal to undertake the enormously complicated task of completing the system's transition into the historical era that began some twenty-five or thirty years ago. The most important aspects of Mikhail S. Gorbachev's vision are his willingness to publicly acknowledge the severity of his country's ailments and his awareness that all the principal spheres of the system must be analyzed in tandem and reformed simultaneously. He knows that the economy alone cannot be the link that will haul the whole chain. Society, culture, the state, the party, and the economy—all will have to to be reformed with some degree of coordination, responding to the structural demands of the present historical stage.

As the passing months have demonstrated to skeptics inside and outside the USSR, Gorbachev is in dead earnest and his government is not about to fall. If anything, the "new strategic orientation," as Soviet leaders have labeled it, has become stronger throughout 1987. Week by week, almost, the leadership seems better able to calculate how broad the sweep of reform must be. As their insights and reasoning become more complex, the tasks before them multiply and seem almost impossible to accomplish, and yet the very breadth of their vision makes the entire enterprise more realistic and credible.

We must understand that we are witnessing the beginning of an era of reform that will need at least two "five-year plans" to express itself fully. What is brewing today in the Soviet Union is one of the most intriguing phenomena of our times. So much is being proclaimed, launched, and undertaken that we must talk not only of Gorbachev's policies but of a "Gorbachev phenomenon," even if we cannot yet explain how serious it all is or where it is going.

Indeed, experts should apply caution in providing such explanations at this point. It is too soon even to formulate the correct questions about the intensity, durability, and direction of the Gorbachev phenomenon. First, we must try to understand the changes that took place before Gorbachev came to power. Thus although I discuss some of the potential of the reform movement in the second part of this book, I devote far more attention to pointing out the changes that have, over the last several decades, brought about a new Soviet social reality. This new social environment, in turn, has created a host of serious problems, the persistent pressures to solve them, and the people ready to propose the necessary solutions—including Gorbachev.

A final caution. By now the slogan *glasnost'* has become familiar almost the world over, and its prevalence has begun to create perhaps a false sense of clarity. We must realize that our understanding of the Soviet Union is inadequate and that the complexity of the emerging situation cannot be encapsulated in one or two slogans. As glasnost continues, we are introduced to unfamiliar aspects of Soviet life: cultural and ideological diversity, the tensions between dynamism and sloth, the desiderata of the proponents and opponents of reform. Surely, the USSR is revealing itself to be far less monolithic and homogeneous than we ever suspected.

This novel situation baffles most Soviet politicians, intellectuals, and publics as well. Soviet participants and onlookers are divided into groups that remain indifferent, resigned, or worried, groups that support, oppose, or actively combat the new leadership. Not a few sympathizers fear and most opponents of reform hope that the freedoms just granted can be taken away. Setbacks, "rotten compromises" or even a plain sellout is predicted. Others argue that change is catching on and that the public is responding favorably. Whatever the final outcome, the new political complexion of the Soviet Union will take at least a decade to emerge from this intricate interplay of forces and opinions. No one can foresee Russia's future. The old system is still in place and its supporters, deeply disturbed by the perestroika, will certainly resist change. The reformers are not assured of victory: they will have to fight hard for it, go for bold new moves. Their failure would be terribly costly for the USSR and could well produce negative repercussions worldwide. The world is now watching Moscow attentively and with good reason.

It is a pleasure to express my appreciation to the capable team of editors at the University of California

Press who made my work as an author so much easier. Sheila Levine convinced me to write this book at a time when I was planning something else. Mary Lamprech and Lillian Robyn harnessed all the production resources of the press. Amy Einsohn did a remarkable job of editing the rough manuscript into a legible text. Of course, the opinions and shortcomings of the book are mine alone.

—August 1987

Prefatory Note for the Second Edition

For the second edition, I have written the two new chapters that compose Part Three. Parts One and Two, as well as the Introduction and Bibliography, are reprinted without any substantive changes, though a few minor errors have been corrected.

—June 1990

Introduction

The Soviet Union may be on the verge of important changes in the way it conducts its affairs, maybe even in the way it is run.* Since Mikhail S. Gorbachev became general secretary in March 1985, news from Moscow is ever more startling. Although Western observers admit that things look extremely promising, they are rather skeptical, if not baffled, for many, among whom the U.S. specialists are the most influential, do not believe that the USSR can produce meaningful social, economic, or political change. They expect Gorbachev to continue his tinkering, but predict only protracted stagnation for a system whose possibilities have been exhausted.

Such a widespread attitude cannot easily be faulted. In the 1950s the startling destalinization undertaken by Nikita S. Khrushchev was blocked, even pushed back to some extent, and many hopes were raised and then frustrated. The spate of economic reforms enacted under Aleksei N. Kosygin in the 1960s failed to substantially change the sluggish economic system. "Thaws" in cultural life have invariably been followed by "freezes." Why take this newest thaw more seriously than the earlier ones?

And yet, this time the skeptics and naysayers may be

---

*This was written in February 1987. By January 1990, the hypothetical "maybe" is already too timid. [M.L., January 1990] overlooking something crucial. Khrushchev's destalinization was, in fact, thwarted, but restalinization did not occur. Kosygin's economic reforms failed, but they left ongoing economic experiments, bequeathed an unrepudiated concept of a "socialist market" and a potent economic science, especially of the mathematical variety, with new scholars, institutes, and experts ready to bounce back once circumstances would permit. The literary and artistic scene, even without new official thaws, continued a respectful and quite variegated activity, conquering new positions—officially, semiofficially, and unofficially—changing the cultural realm profoundly and earning at least a de facto acceptance. And in the ideological sphere new orientations appeared and began to flourish in the different publics, including in official circles. Yet Western thinking about the USSR all too rarely acknowledges that there is more to Soviet life than just Marxism-Leninism.

More seriously, the aforementioned changes have been pointing to something deeper in the making. In a recent, very revealing book, the British journalist Martin Walker puts his finger on the relevant broader issue. "The country," Walker writes, "went through a social revolution while Brezhnev slept" [108:175]. If this is true, many observers were napping together with Leonid I. Brezhnev. "The sovietological profession," complained a colleague, Professor Stephen F. Cohen, in a recent conversation, "was not ready for Gorbachev."

Here, let me simply summarize some of the reasons for this situation, based on arguments I have presented in earlier writings [62:4–5].

The prevailing conception that has taken a firm hold in the field of Soviet studies is "totalitarianism," denoting the idea of a terroristic government seeking total control of the population by massive use of indoctrination, police and ideological brainwashing, monopoly of sources of information and exercise of power as well as direct control over the economy. According to this model, the state marshals its powers to preclude any autonomy of organization and expression, cultural or other, unless authorized. The label "totalitarian" was used to describe such regimes as Nazi Germany under Hitler and Soviet Russia under Stalin, and the term did seem to serve some cognitive purpose. But, as is well known, during the cold war the term was appropriated in the West for propagandist and ideological use in the service of strategic competition. The odium inherent in the term was transferred from the previous foe—Nazi Germany—to the new one, Soviet Russia. At the same time, influential sovietologists, not at all innocent of the ideological content of the undertaking, tried to make totalitarianism look like an explanatory, theoretical concept that offers the public and the student a tool for understanding the system in question.

Though the term served quite well in its ideological function, it was useless as a conceptual category. It did not have much to say about where the system came from, where it was heading, what kind of changes it was undergoing, if any, and how to study it critically and seriously. In fact, the term was, in this context, itself "totalitarian" in its empty self-sufficiency: it did not recognize any mechanism of change in the Soviet Union and had no use for even a shadow of some historical process.

All in all, Western perceptions of the Soviet Union and its prospects were seriously hampered by a cognitive schema that prevented practitioners from seeing the world in a realistic way. Through the 1960s a considerable number of Western scholars finally abandoned this ideologically biased tool, and serious scholarly efforts, notably by economists, political sociologists, and historians, were undertaken, enriching our understanding. But, on the whole, these analyses shared one important assumption with the "totalitarian school": the focus remained the study of the state and the state-run economy, to the exclusion of most other aspects of Soviet experience.

Studying the Soviet state is, of course, a must. But the launching of the five-year plans and the making of Stalinism in the 1930s made the state loom so large that observers were easily misled into taking the state as the main, if not the sole, actor in the history of the system. A one-party regime, a state-owned economy, harsh ideological and police controls, overall bureaucratization of life, a powerful leadership, and, in one crucial period, an omnipotent absolutist ruler—those were facts and it was perhaps tempting to assume that studying such essentials would deliver the key to the whole order. Justified as these impressions were, they nevertheless led to conceptually flawed conclusions and produced a misleadingly incomplete picture. Here was something quite ahistorical: A political system without a social one, a state floating over everything else, over history itself. Such a state submitted only to its own laws, was explainable only in its own terms. Efforts to figure out what such "laws" might be could not move beyond rules of immutability, stagnation, or fixity. If change was posited as possible, it was conceived of as small variations within the unalterable framework; that such a state could undergo serious reform seemed unthinkable.

Their attention held fast, most analysts completely neglected the key ideas and key parts of any nation's historical reality. The rich and complex social fabric of the

USSR was very little studied; Soviet culture and the countercultures and subcultures that shape minds, attitudes, and expectations were largely ignored. And the interrelation of society and culture with the economy, the state, and the party remained unexplored. Yet precisely such concepts had to be worked out if we wanted to speak intelligently about historical events.

In sum, what had been missing was the idea of a Soviet "social system" and, in turn, the conceptualization of a dynamic historical process in which all the subsystems interact in time and space, yielding ever more complex and intricate patterns.

Because Soviet society has not been studied in all its manifestations, the Soviet historical experience continues to be poorly understood. And until broadened perspectives enter into Western thinking about the USSR, constant and costly errors of judgment will be made, crises will be overblown or noticed at the eleventh hour, and sources of strength and vigor will go unobserved. How much longer can Western scholars, politicians, and strategists afford to have "their" Russia served up as simplistically as possible?

A few fundamental and hopefully useful ideas can be proposed without overreaching, at this stage, for any grand theories. Regardless of how one defines a social system—the general literature on the subject is quite voluminous—one has to dispose of the idea that it may be weak and ineffectual because society is either "atomized"—as many contended about the Soviet Union, especially under Stalin—or is poorly integrated because of enormous social disparities, as Paul Miliukov maintained about tsarist society.

Though such terms are clearly applicable in particular cases, any society so described at times displays a vigor and cohesion that belies the term applied. Thus such notions do not enable us to make much headway. Social disparities, social strife, and social chasms do not prevent an aggregate, a social system, from forming and impinging upon all its parts. The palaces of nobility and peasants' huts, the glitter of capitals and the squalor of abject slums, the worlds of literacy and illiteracy, of power and helplessness, taken together form a system. Political events and economy, roads and trains, schools and churches, tax collectors and armies, receiving wages or rendering services—are all powerful, often unrecognized links that produce a historical entity. Even a loose imbrication is still an interconnected system. In the absence of such understanding of a social system, all one can do is interpret crises, revolutionary changes of systems and structures, as mere accidents begotten by the stupidity of a king, a queen, or a fool.

States, however despotic, are part of the historical entity, powerful yet subjected to pressures, to corrosive influences, stemming from independent, outside factors or resulting from the state's own actions. These internal and external pressures can produce quick, often rather unexpected effects, such as loss of vigor in the ruling groups, debilitating economic crises, and loss of support in the population or among strategically important elites. In such cases the state, democratic or authoritarian, finds itself in great trouble and has to change or go.

Just such events have taken place in Soviet history, and we will see how even this "atomized" society, disoriented and apparently unable to stand up against a powerful state apparatus, continued to prescribe limits and constraints that had to be recognized by the nation's leadership. Should a regime fail to observe such limits, the leaders themselves would pay for it, or else a heavy price might be exacted from the country that would discredit the regime, corrupt and weaken it.

Such an approach, more exacting but fruitful, allows us to grasp general trends of development that almost always lead a system in directions quite different from where state leaders want to go. After all, planners do not plan difficulties, imbalances, and crises, but they still get them, quite often.

One final conceptual point. The usual antithesis of "state" versus "society" may be inadequate when one wants to explore relations between the two. If one accepts the argument that states, however arbitrary, are part of a larger whole and cannot remain arbitrary without catastrophic results, one needs to work from a conceptualization of the state that allows one to grasp the connections between the political and other areas of social life.

A state is a carrier of a set of coercive and integrative functions, changing in time and space, but executed by an array of institutions that can be called "government." These institutions are helped by others that are not part of the government; for example, political parties that supply leaders and personnel for governmental bodies, or private armament producers who are closely and directly involved with the government. Thus "the state" is a subsystem comprising both governmental and nongovernmental institutions.

Next comes a welter of institutions, neither government nor state, but without which societal functions and the legitimacy of the state will be faulty or wanting. Here we have trade unions, churches, the media, and organizations of all kinds that agree to support the system. Together with the state these groups are components of a broader entity: the political system. It is on this canvas that the states relations with social factors are worked out, mended, or strained. Such a three-tier conceptual ladder—government, state, and political system—allows us to reason about cases when a weak state still does not endanger a strong political system; when an obviously fragile, unsupportive, or restive political system may be shored up by a strong state; when a poor government, even if allowed to stay on, can be afforded by a strong state or a strong polity.

The introduction of social and societal factors into our reasoning allows us to see Soviet history and state institutions as much more flexible and responsive to social realities than is generally perceived. We can then begin to examine the richness and complexity of Soviet history, the stages through which the system transited as well as the character of the current situation. Stalinism, the vexed problem of Soviet history, may also become more amenable to analysis and interpretation.

In sum, the USSR is more complex, richer and much more of a challenge to students, hiding still more than one trick up its sleeve from the unsuspecting and the ill-advised. To restrict our analytic arsenal to simplified and, for the most part, quite inadequate ideas, is a prescription for constant failure of intellect and politics. If an inventory were drawn up of the main assessments and predictions by academics, the media, and politicians at different, often crucial turning points in Soviet history, surely the balance would not be positive. Not just Hitler, but also Western leaders and the military expected Russia to collapse quickly during World War II. At Stalin's death many expected another Stalin, and it was argued quite often that the Soviet system could not function in any other way. Since then, one hears again and again that the Soviet government is unstable, that it teeters at every change of a general secretary, that it cannot handle succession. (Indeed, this assertion was still a cornerstone of press reports at a time when three new general secretaries took over the position, each time in a matter of days.)

But most of these misconceptions are trifles compared to the widespread misperception of an inherent weakness stemming from an almost sclerotic institutional grid that cannot but be what it is and, finally, is destined to go under.

Let us instead proceed from the assumption that the Soviet historical process has been, and continues to be, full of twists and turns, changes of form and substance. We will then begin to understand that far from being anything "finished," Russia is now entering a crucial new stage and is therefore, in many respects, just a beginner.

Part
One

From Village to Megacity—
A Country in a Hurry

1

The Rural Dimension,
from the Tsars to Stalin

Indispensable to our understanding of either the longer stretch of Russian/Soviet history or its most recent leg is an appreciation of the crucial role of agriculture and the peasantry. And any study of the rural sector in the modern period must take into account over two hundred years of efforts to accelerate economic development, starting from the times of Peter the Great. Throughout this period, the agrarian system weighed heavily on Russia, and the transformation of this system took several revolutions and costly, dramatic convulsions.

In theory, economic development may be promoted "from above," by the state or some of its leaders, or it may be taken up and followed up by social initiative, with or without state help. The classic examples of development from above are the policies of Peter the Great, followed by others equally well known. In contrast, during the last decades of tsarist Russia much of the initiative came from the emerging entrepreneurial classes. But whatever the pattern of development, the state is either an advocate or an obstacle; the state is either coping well, weathering crises that result from the accelerated economic development, or it is not coping and eventually falls apart. In a nutshell, all such hypothetical outcomes were fulfilled at various times in Russian history.

Despite the vigorous economic and cultural advances that followed the emancipation of the peasants, and which continued, impressively, until World War I, tsarist Russia remained an agrarian system and state. The bulk of the population continued to be engaged in agriculture of a mostly primitive type, at a time when in the West a technologic and scientific revolution had long been working economic and social marvels. But most Russian landowners, the other part of the agrarian system, did not manage to transform their domains into modern enterprises, preferring to use the abundant and cheap labor of a mass of poor peasants who worked as sharecroppers or debtors, not as wage earners.

Obviously, this rather unproductive agrarian base could not offer enough resources to finance a hectic development, and the growing needs of the state constantly strained the peasants' ability to carry the burdens. Those are well-known facts. For our purposes we have to examine briefly the sociopolitical context of Tsardom. The same landowning class that did not show much ability to manage its estates profitably was also the political ruling class: they were at the top of the government bureaucracy, as well as dominant in the tsarist courts, where crucial policy decisions were made.

We can thus talk of a social pattern, composed of the peasantry, landowners (*dvoriane*), and the royal court, with the tsar at its head, that also was still the political and economic reality of tsardom. The waves of capitalist expansion, the appearance of important industrial and financial centers, which through market relations penetrated far corners of the empire and promised to transform the economy and society, did not go far enough or deep enough. The "rural nexus"—a term I have used in a recent work [62:12]—did not easily dissolve. Perched on this kind of nexus and reflecting it, the tsarist state could not reform fast enough to deal with the developmental tasks or, notably, with the requirements of warfare.

The revolution and civil war destroyed the old system and created a different kind of state. The social composition of the leadership, the personnel of governmental institutions, together with the very character of the system changed drastically (even if specialists and professionals from the previous era were still needed for their expertise). The new revolutionary ideology was, unlike that of the previous regime, deeply committed to industrialization and economic development. But, paradoxically, postrevolutionary Russia, during Lenin's New Economic Policy (NEP), was even more rural, and equally—if not more—backward than tsarist Russia. The urban population, by official count, merely returned to its prewar share of the total. A more exacting evaluation shows convincingly that no more than 16 percent of the people were city dwellers, leaving 84 percent in the countryside and dependent on a low-yielding agriculture [14:27–30].

Furthermore, during the revolution the peasants took over all lands that had belonged to landowners and to some richer peasants and thereby destroyed most of the market-oriented sectors of agriculture. The resulting ocean of small family farms was owned and organized under a complex, communal-cum-homestead system. The farmers' mediocre output—meant mainly for home consumption—left little to spare for the cities and the state, and the capitalist inroads made possible by the reforms of the tsarist Prime Minister Piotr Arkadevich Stolypin were wiped out. The peasantry thus settled into a more archaic mode of life and production that imposed on the whole country the dilemmas of what is known today as underdevelopment. Indeed, a reputable Soviet sociologist, Iu. Arutiunian, considered the USSR in the 1920s to be at almost the same level as India and Egypt, for the combined effects of the civil war and the agrarian revolution had produced a dangerous economic backslide, as evidenced by most of the vital indices of the system. If the prerevolutionary society Lenin's government took over was backward enough, its problems were aggravated by the Civil War that wiped out many of the advanced social, cultural, and economic sectors of tsarist Russia. In sum, "archaization" [62:18] seems quite suitable to characterize the postrevolutionary situation, except for the emergence of a new agency in power—the party.

The mass of peasants now weighed more heavily on the new system than on the previous regime, notably because they restored to full dominance their communal arrangements, previously on the wane. The redistribution of land to peasants according to the number of mouths to feed in each family served a principle of justice befitting the peasants' way of life and need of survival, but it served less well the national need for agricultural productivity.

We have in mind here the famous peasant commune, the "mir," similar to ancient rural organizations elsewhere. These mirs Marx characterized as "localized microcosms," adding that this type of organization does not occur everywhere but when it does "it erects over such [communities] a more or less centralized despotism" [66:405].

Lenin concurred, referring to the Russian peasantry as constituting "a massive and simple patriarchal foundation of the tsarist monarchy." At least, that is, until the 1905 revolution awakened those peasants from their "deep political slumber" [97:141]. In 1917 the peasantry again became politicized, but it soon fell back into its "slumber" and left Lenin with the bill to pay. He found himself in the clutches of a historical reality that had been created, to a large extent, by the system of "localized microcosms" that forced the state, reluctantly at first, with considerable relish thereafter, to erect "a more or less centralized despotism." The job to be done, however, for which the new state was bracing itself, was not of the type more ancient despotisms were called to do.

Obviously, these events were crucial in making the new system and directing its historical destiny. To understand the next stages in Soviet history, we need at this juncture to borrow some concepts from the thought-provoking work of Fernand Braudel. In his analysis of the eighteenth century, when the economy in the West was still predominantly preindustrial, Braudel discerned three basic layers in socioeconomic life. The mass of people lived on the bottom layer, in a system of elementary "material life." Above this layer was emerging a "market economy," which was complex but still correlated in many ways with the more primitive subsoil. The third layer, "capitalism," was depicted by Braudel as an external force, different in scale, methods, and substance, from the other two. In due course, capitalism would deeply transform the two lower layers, imposing itself on them from above [10:112].

Braudel also emphasized that the slower-moving, more primitive layers were deeply hostile to the faster-moving forces of modern growth. The peasantry, he maintained, and the small-scale market mechanisms serving it, on the one hand, and the dynamic forces of capitalism, on the other, "were two universes, two ways of life foreign to each other."

When we look at twentieth-century Russia, Braudel's three socioeconomic layers are clearly discernible, especially once the topmost layer was in effect dislodged by the Russian Revolution. Indeed, in a situation unique in this part of the world, revolutionary events could "peel off" the capitalist layer, because it was still a separate layer that had not yet had the chance to replow the economy and society as it had in the West. But then the new state had to face the country's enormous, primeval social and economic life, represented mainly by a peasantry oriented toward basic subsistence. It was up to this state now to do the job capitalism did elsewhere: to create large-scale enterprises and industrial, scientific, and cultural forms—all quite foreign to the experience of the small-scale rural worlds. In doing so, the state unavoidably inherited the tensions and hostility between "the two universes."

Facing the stubborn routine of the peasantry—a world with which the upper echelons had little in common and one that the lower officialdom wanted to quit as soon as possible—was not going to be an easy task for the new and ambitious state. Staffed largely by cadres of popular extraction, the state was torn between the tendency to move slowly and cautiously or, alternatively, to exert powerful pressure from above. Lack of communication with the other "universe" accounts for the latter tendency, but also the fear that the rural world, the world of small-scale producers and of small-scale markets, would reproduce the capitalism that the revolution had just abolished.

Lenin contributed to these fears by his statement,

made during the civil war, that the countryside was producing capitalism every hour, every day.* It may well be
that he changed his mind at the end of his life, but in any
case, it is doubtful that Marx would have agreed with
this analysis. Whereas Lenin and others in his party
feared "markets," Marx (in a statement that Braudel
would have liked but apparently didn't know) stated
that "production of goods and their circulation is no
more than a premise for the capitalist mode of production." Further, Marx held that capitalism could emerge
only after a division of labor had developed, a division
"possible only on the base of cities where there is a great
concentration and density of population, differentiation
of its activities and [a high level of] intercourse" [15:31].

So, according to Marx, the breeding ground of any
capitalist menace was not the countryside, but the cities.
Another great authority, Max Weber, offered an even
more sweeping statement in his book on medieval cities.
For him urban development, while not alone decisive,
was a carrier of both capitalism and the state [109:181].
We can add that, under favorable conditions, cities also
promoted a third phenomenon, democracy.

Despite such authorities, the approach among Soviet
leaders, based on a fear of the countryside as the source
of capitalism, prevailed—at least in the ideological discourse. In fact, the problem was the peasant *tout court*.

All these facts and concepts go some way toward helping us to grasp the character of the Soviet system, the
terms that defined its stages of development and even, to
some extent, its prospect in the future.

---

*Lenin used stronger wording: insofar as the peasant farm re-
mained a small-scale commodity producer, it "engendered capitalism and the bourgeoisie permanently, every day, every hour, sponta-
neously and massively" (V. I. Lenin, *Polnoe Sobranie sochinenii*
[Moscow, 1963], 41:6).

Thus at Soviet Russia's point of entry into the NEP, the country was still saddled with a version of the agrarian nexus. No court, no gentry anymore, but an agrarian economy and a huge muzhik ocean. Though the urban sector was expected to serve as a springboard for further advances, it still was, before and after the revolution, deeply embedded in rural society. Most cities were small, and their rural origins and connections with the country were highly visible. The occupations, ethos, and way of life of many city-dwellers bore deep similarities with the prevailing peasant models: small-scale family businesses, traditional festivals and mores, high rates of illiteracy—all quite well documented by ethnographers [4:63–87]. Data reported by the noted Soviet demographer V. Ts. Urlanis about tsarist cities before World War I were still valid for the Soviet period under the NEP: Most of the houses in the cities were built of timber; only one third had iron roofs, one third had timber roofs, and one quarter had thatched roofs. Half the cities had no library of any kind, and 95 percent had no institutions of higher education [105:44–45]. Though this semiurban branch of the rural world kept developing into new directions, whenever new waves of migrants arrived from the villages a considerable "ruralization" often occurred—to which many cities easily succumbed.

Evidently, the bigger cities, especially the capitals, were better able to resist such waves. They created and kept reproducing, even spreading, models of a genuine urban civilization. Yet they were still, under the tsar as well as under Lenin, just islands in the muzhik ocean.

The next period in Soviet history was to become crucial for the future of the country and was to pose an extremely complicated problem for the national conscience. This period began in 1928 with a dramatic change of policies in reaction to old problems coupled with a crisis, one of several, in the vital flow of grain supplies. The new policy showed the state's ability to muster its institutions and whatever public support was available into a program for accelerated economic growth. The subsequent "big drive" changed the entire country and the political system quite profoundly. It produced a new state model, some of whose features became fixed in the system, while others subsided or disappeared in later decades. This set of policies and patterns, usually referred to as "stalinism," accomplished what any government of this type would hope to, but it also relied on terror of an unprecedented scale. A vast complex of police forces and concentration camps—certainly a key feature of this system—was crowned by a peculiar (some think, peculiarly oriental) brand of personal absolutism exercised by the general secretary.

It is not easy to discern any rationale for the mass imprisonments and murders during the great purges of the late 1930s. And the explanation of such events will not be found in any such rationale. Rather, to explore this phenomenon, we must begin by reconsidering the agrarian nexus, the prevailing social landscape. As noted earlier, the effects of the country's backwardness were compounded by the archaization of the system as a result of events between 1914 and 1921. Clearly this backsliding clouded the prospects of the regime, but it also left the state as the sole potent actor capable of mobilizing scarce social, cultural, and economic resources in the service of a program for change. A combination of state bureaucracies and the specific agency called "party" produces the leaders, entrepreneurs, educators, and indoctrinators during the leap forward of the 1930s. But a mechanism parallel to the one that destroyed the tsarist regime then came into play, as the powerful developmental thrust into rural society caused a protracted social crisis. A series of furious economic, educational, and military undertakings shook up and restructured society, affected all its social classes, and thereby caused havoc in the system. Sudden changes of social position, occupation, status, and location operated on such a scale as to create a "quicksand society" [62:221] characterized by flux, uncertainty, mobility, high turnover, and anomie.

The resulting chaos, especially in the early 1930s, much of it creative, much unexpected and damaging, is an important historical factor. The system was supposedly planned and administered, and much was, in fact, tightly controlled. But although the government tried to dominate the work and movement of people, there was also at play an enormous spontaneity and drift. An unprecedented, quite spontaneous influx into the cities of about 27 million people (in a decade), to mention only those who not merely visited but stayed, brought a new, awesome wave of "ruralization" to the cities, the working class, and parts of the bureaucracy.

Bureaucratization is the other relevant phenomenon. It was growing by leaps and bounds, but this social and political product was crumbly, as one would expect from such sudden growth in the absence of an adequate and timely supply of necessary cadres. Although in due course a modernized Soviet bureaucracy would abolish the stalinist police-autocracy, at this stage the cadres were extremely disoriented (not unlike the whole social system at the time) and not yet "modern" at all. They were most often self-made, quickly "baked," promoted en masse to ever more complex jobs. No doubt the rapid advancement was an exhilarating novelty for them, but certainly they needed more time and instruction to learn how to handle those jobs and conduct themselves in the new environment. It is no exaggeration to see the cadres of these years, with some notable exceptions, basically as *praktiki*, that is, responsible, often top-level cadres in political, social, technological, and even cultural positions whose training was inadequate or nonexistent; they learned as they went along.

It is neither possible nor necessary here to trace the stages of Stalin's ascension to supreme power. (There is a good literature on this period, although we are still uninformed about many of its aspects.) But it is clear that this period of social upheaval and crisis sorely overtaxed the freshly promoted, still unstable bureaucracy, and that the struggling bureaucracy's shortcomings and lack of experience presented a particularly propitious ground for the usurpation of power at the top—by a dictator and at lower levels by despotic bosses. The displacement of power was easily effected at the broad layers of the government bureaucracy, though it took somewhat longer to happen inside the party.

The making of a despot thus reflected the inability of society and the bureaucracy to establish some rules for the government. This vacuum invited an arbitrary and capricious use of power and a paranoid interpretation of, and reaction to, what was happening in the country. The bureaucratic apparatus created to dam the flood, to overcome the social crisis, found itself in a crisis of its own and then threw itself into the arms of a miracle-worker with an appetite for ruling.

While Stalin often blamed the failures of the system on "sabotage," the disorder among the population was a normal reaction of a hard-pressed, disoriented body social trying to defend itself and cope with everyday problems and tasks. Such predictable spontaneity, however, was deeply unsettling when seen from above. Misunderstanding the character of spontaneity and thus fearing it, the police-autocracy inflicted retribution on the masses of people.

By now we have come to realize how feverish and almost chaotic was the large-scale restructuring undertaken during those years. In particular, the process of state building has been deeply affected by the social phenomena of the 1930s. We have in mind here the resurgence, again, in a new and peculiar form, of the rural nexus. This time the poorly collectivized peasants were flanked by millions of poorly urbanized ones, and they were ruled by a mass of bureaucratic *praktiki*, many of whom, at least in the lower ranks, were also partly of rural or semirural origin. Such was the social background of the regime in those years. Confronted by the baffling sequels to its policies, the regime resorted, out of despair, but mostly by inclination, to methods that corrupted the state system. The resulting pathology was soon sanctified by a dogma produced for the occasion, and the improvisation of the 1930s hardened into patterns that were bequeathed to Stalin's heirs.

Still, stalinism turned out to be a passing phenomenon. That is one provisional conclusion we can make at this stage. The civil war produced one pattern of rule, the NEP another, and yet another emerged under Stalin. They are species of the same genus, no doubt, but the differences are quite striking. Social change and structure are the crucial factors, for each change of key parameters of the social structure—around the turn of the century before the revolution, after the civil war, and in the early

1930s—was followed by changes in the outlook, composition, and methods of political institutions, as I have argued in detail elsewhere [62:21–26].

The power of the state under Stalin, however harsh the controls and the dictatorship, could not thwart the force and impact of spontaneous social developments. In the social sphere a persistent and irresistible autonomy gathered its own momentum, posed reactions to state actions, and created many unpredictable results. For no matter how stern or cruel a regime, in the laboratory of history only rarely can state coercion be so powerful as to control fully the course of events. The depth and scope of spontaneous events that counter the wishes and expectations of a dictatorial government are not a lesser part of history than the deeds and misdeeds of the government and the state.

To illustrate these contentions, let us consider the main social groups during the stalinist period. Workers, for instance, reacted to the worsening conditions of life by learning and applying the techniques of self-defense: the turnover rate soared and labor discipline plummeted. Widespread connivance between managers and their labor forces proved to be ineradicable, despite official efforts to instil or coerce discipline and productivity. When authorities did achieve some success in pressuring cooperation but did not propose the improvements that workers expected, a new "front" would open up against procedures and norms, mostly by tacit agreement, without any organizers or leaders, just by a barely visible wink. This was a constant battle, with victories and defeats for both sides.

The same applies to the peasants in kolkhozy. Their reactions to collectivization included a massive slaughter of cattle, the flight to cities or construction sites, and endless strategems to beat the system. Great zeal was shown in working on the private plots, little zeal displayed in working in the collectivized fields. On many points, the government finally had to yield: the granting to kolkhoz families of the right to a private plot and a cow is one well-known example. In any case, the state never got from the kolkhozy all it really wanted. The pressure of the peasants managed to transform the kolkhoz into a hybrid organization that was nothing like what state authorities had hoped for.

The bureaucracy is yet another case in point. Although the state gave orders and expected their execution, it never truly mastered this social group. For the bureaucrats, too, had their techniques of self-defense: they knew how to conceal realities and performances, how to help each other get jobs during interminable contractions of staffs (which nevertheless kept growing). In a word, the bureaucracy never became the pliable tool it was expected to be. Purges and persecutions only lowered the bureaucracy's performance, sharpened the "creativity" of its defensive techniques, and intensified the lobbying and pressuring of superiors.

Indeed, whatever field, function, or action we study, we discover that the government's battle for its programs, plans, and objectives always encountered social reaction, drift, spontaneity, and the powerful force of inertia.

In the field of culture, for example, various social groups accepted certain values preferred and propagandized by the government, but they also created their own countercultures or subcultures. Every official slogan, song, or even speech by Stalin was immediately paraphrased and parodied, sung or recited by students, soldiers, and peasants all over the country. The camps that were supposed to isolate the population from all kinds of "enemies of the people" produced an enormous output of texts and songs, some of them deeply gloomy and hooligan in style, some of a political character. These lampoons and scornful satires stalked the country despite the fact that no media were at their disposal other than word-of-mouth communication. Everywhere people made barbed jokes and witticisms, thousands of them, that were irreverent, uncensorable, often punishable by a minimum of five years in a labor camp—and indomitable.

Ideological indoctrination was not ineffective—far from it—but it wasn't fully effective either. People could listen attentively with one ear, and let the message pass through the other. Re-education was successful only up to a certain point, depending on the character of the social group and its filters. Some slogans were accepted, if they did not seriously contradict the listeners' perception of reality. Social, economic, and cultural developments signaled to the population, sometimes sooner than to the authorities, what life was really about. But the authorities complained constantly that people did not go where asked, found ways of doing things their own way, exploited any loophole to play or outplay the system, and helped themselves through networks of friends, acquaintances, briberies, and adventurous risks.

The idea that the Russians and the other nationalities of the USSR are unquestioningly obedient and are easy to rule is a pipe dream. I could cite many government decisions and orders, sternly worded, that no one paid any attention to. Aware that it was losing the fight, the government resorted to the ultimate tool that denotes frustration and ineptitude: terror. Sometimes even terror had no effect or produced results contrary to the perpetrators' intention. Every state measure, control system, interdiction or exhortation provoked some sort of battle, quite often a losing one. Some things worked: many, sooner or later, didn't. The internal passport system, for instance, was introduced to control the movements of, in particular, the peasant population. But it could not stop spontaneous and unwanted migrations: peasants continued to move into cities, where growth was to be controlled, and out of the kolkhozy, where they were badly needed.

Should we ever see the memoirs of people who really knew Stalin, surely we would hear of him often repeating the well-known statement about an ancient, frustrated Russian prince: "Monomakh's hat is very heavy indeed." (*Tiazhela shapka Monomakha*, referring to Prince Vladimir Monomakh of the twelfth century.)

Often the state got what it wanted, but at the price of being considerably derailed or rerouted. The train of history is not really a train. The engineer guides it into some station, yet the train arrives somewhere else. All this, without organized opposition, open or clandestine, and without any widespread political dissent. Simply the work of the laboratory of history, in which more takes place than the mere obeying of orders.

Let me conclude this review of the spontaneous effects and acts that shadowed the dictatorial and powerful state at every step and "corrected" or frustrated it by simply mentioning the phenomenon that is at the center of my argument: urbanization itself. The growth of even the capitals was very much a spontaneous development, yet the cities eventually turned out to be the main engine of Russia's most momentous social—and soon, probably also political—transformation.

The study of Russian and Soviet history must be conducted on these lines, especially when dealing with Stalin. For he is entirely undecipherable if one ignores the structural constraints and spontaneous actions and reactions of society.

Were it otherwise, states and dictators could really "plan" or drag history according to their own designs; they would not only master individuals and whole groups but also run the entire historical game. The world is, unfortunately, not immune to despotism and to oppressive states—but, fortunately, no state has ever figured out how to master the complexity of human society for longer than a limited time span.

2

The Rise of the Cities

Various factors trigger and sustain the creation of urban settlements and an urban system: industrialization, first and foremost, and such developments as educational and scientific achievements, the growth of administrations, and the momentum of urban society itself once it takes root and manifests its potentials. But for our purposes it is the outcome of these undertakings that is our key theme and focus. From the demographic data concerning the growth of Soviet urban society in the last half century much can be inferred about the series of deep transformations the USSR went through and about the latest, crucial stage in which it finds itself today.

The pace of Soviet urban development in the 1930s, its scope, intensity, and speed, was described by the American geographer Chauncy Harris as "record breaking" [29:239]. The urban population grew at an annual rate of 6.5 percent between 1926 and 1939, peaking at an annual rate of over 10 percent in the later thirties. Concurrently, the urban share of the USSR's population rose from 18 percent to over 32 percent. Such an increase, Harris notes, required three decades in the United States, from 1856 to 1887 [29:240]. He might have added that in the Soviet case these percentage shifts represented far greater numbers of people: in the 1930s the Soviet urban population grew from 26.3 million to 56.1 million. Many new cities were created, and many others saw their populations double or triple in twelve years. Further, these figures include only those people who permanently settled in the cities. Millions of others arrived in towns and cities only to soon wander away or run away, according to their circumstances.

Such a degree of social flux could not but trigger crises and mutations. But let us follow the story into the postwar period, when the USSR crossed the threshold of urbanization. In 1960 the urban population accounted for 49 percent of the total; by 1972 urban dwellers outnumbered rural dwellers, 58 percent to 42 percent.* Between 1972 and 1985 the dominantly urban Soviet society became almost predominantly urban, accounting for 65 percent of the total population and 70 percent of the population of the RSFSR. Today over 180 million Soviet citizens live in cities—compared to 56 million just before World War II.

Urbanization has entailed both the vigorous creation of new settlements and the expansion of old ones. The most recent intercensus period, 1959 to 1980, shows an

---

*In comparison, the urban sector passed the 50 percent mark in the U.S. in 1921. France almost reached it in 1911, but experienced a slowdown and finally crossed this threshold, with some difficulty, between 1925 and 1931 [19:20]. Germany had already reached the 65 percent mark by 1925—a meaningful pointer to events that were to unfold.

increase in all categories of towns, townships, and settlements, but of particular importance are the bigger cities:

Population	Number of Soviet Cities	
	1959	1980
100,000 to 250,000	88	163
250,000 to 500,000	34	65
1,000,000+	3	23

All in all, in 1980 some 272 Soviet cities had more than 100,000 inhabitants (compared to only 89 cities in 1939), and these cities are now home to almost half of the urban population and about one third of the total population of the country.

That one fourth of the nation's people live in the biggest cities testifies not only to a powerful process of urbanization but also to an internal regrouping of the inhabitants in favor of the biggest agglomerations. Some of the smallest towns are struggling, but many are quite dynamic, including those labeled "settlements of urban character," a category pertaining to settlements of different sizes that have not received the status of cities but whose populations are employed predominantly in nonagricultural pursuits. The number of these settlements increased from 2,700 in 1939 to 4,619 in 1959, and to 5,938 by 1980 [48:23].

As these data indicate, the pace of urban formation during the postwar period, especially after 1959, has been quite remarkable. During the last three decades an average of twenty-two new cities were created every year. In this field of social development surely lies one of the most momentous achievements brought about by the Soviet period. Only about 700 cities were chartered by tsarist Russia; today there are over 2,000 formally designated cities. Since the 1930s some 400 cities, by now often big and bustling, were created from scratch, on the site of small villages or on empty terrain. This, despite the fact that much of the decade immediately after World War II was devoted to the task of restoring the hundreds of cities that had been destroyed or badly damaged during the war.

Finally, we may note that in recent years growth in the urban sector has been slowing. Since the 1960s the population of the cities has increased by 3 million a year, partly from internal growth, partly due to migration from rural areas. Between 1959 and 1970, some 1.5 million migrants a year came from villages, even 1.9 million a year in the 1970s. But this influx has tapered off, and in the past ten years it has been the migration from smaller to larger cities that has come to the fore in fashioning the character of the urban phenomenon. The overall size of the urban sector is remaining steady, giving the new complex urban system time to assimilate decades of momentous change. New cities are still being created, especially in Siberia, but everywhere the system and its institutions are, as it were, taking stock.

Thus it is evident that the postwar years, a period of Soviet history that many Western observers characterize as an era of stagnation, actually constitute a period of deep social change. Unfortunately, all too often, the Soviet urban phenomenon has escaped the attention of analysts, with the exception of several books and articles by a few pioneering scholars [28, 29, 63, 67].

But before we consider what Soviet society has become in the wake of its urbanization, we must return again to the countryside. Such backtracking is necessary, from time to time, in order to highlight the novelty and relative immaturity of the phenomenon and to caution against too rosy a view of urbanization.

In discussing the 1930s, I earlier referred to the ruralization of the cities. The flood of peasants to cities old and new was enormous: in the 1930s almost 27 million peasants migrated to towns, doubling the size of the urban population. Although the tide receded, the influx remained considerable and certainly too high for the good of either agriculture or the economy. About 24 million migrants moved to the cities between 1939 and 1959, another 8.4 million between 1959 and 1964, and 16 million between 1964 and 1970. This continual influx of peasants, most of them young people, did not effect a ruralization comparable to that of the 1930s, but the recurrent dilution of urban culture is a social phenomenon of considerable importance. At least during the earlier postwar period of rapid and extensive urbanization, up to 1959, even as the cities quickly became industrial their culture and way of life remained rural [15:149].

The problem is that the rural mind, way of life, and culture are extremely tenacious. It may take some three generations for the peasant outlook and mentality to disappear and for a true urbanite to emerge. This transformation is still in mid process in the Soviet Union today, still an important feature of the social and cultural scene, although subject to considerable regional and national variations. In most cities about half the residents were born in the countryside, half born in the cities [4:58–59]. But by now the balance of reciprocal influence has changed, so that when urban dwellers visit their parents in the villages, they are more likely to leave behind more than they take away. Too, those villagers who often travel to cities are easily recognizable there, but they certainly weigh much less on the ways of the cities than they once did—except for those cities that have many rather recent migrants.

Migration and adaptation to urban life is a difficult and often traumatic process, and is described as such by contemporary Soviet sociologists. This is the case even if the migrant comes from a smaller to a bigger city [91:68]. For the newcomer from a remote rural area, it is like trying to penetrate a fortress without understanding its internal rules. The newcomers face hard times and their psychological resources are heavily tested. But defensive mechanisms appear, consisting of clinging to relatives and *compadres* and sticking to some familiar cultural mechanisms. This is especially obvious in the case of national minorities, who tend to reinforce their ethnic identity so as to better face adversity [92:68–69].

In cases when there is no ethnic difference, a kind of class solidarity emerges among immigrants, a camaraderie based on their origin and their low social position in the new environment. All too often, the newest migrants find themselves at or near the lowest rungs of the social ladder, and some will stay there for the rest of their lives. For that reason, entire districts are to be found in most Soviet cities, especially of recent minting, inhabited by former peasants who are quite identifiable by their outlook and behavior. These fledgling urbanites coalesce into layers that combine properties of class, status, and culture, and they express their identity by adhering to ways carried over from rural traditions [4:33–49]. This type of social coalescence, this re-creation inside the cities of a version of the rural world, may well continue for quite some time in Russia. A similar phenomenon in the history of French urbanization was observed and interpreted by Braudel in his last work [11:235].

Studies of many small towns by Soviet sociologists and ethnographers [4:45] fully justify such assumptions, prompting us to be cautious when assessing the effects of rapid urbanization on the disappearance of rural creeds, mores, and culture. It is precisely the speed of the transformation that may contribute to the preservation of rural culture inside the cities—an obvious defensive mechanism against pervasive urban pressures that the newcomers perceive as destructive.

Where does the sturdiness of the peasant mentality come from?

The tenacity of the peasants' little world—which is being reconstructed by migrants in cities when adaptation to a complicated and hostile environment proves difficult—is a result of a long process of socialization in and by, precisely, the small rural world, the village. Unlike the city, where multifarious influences shape people, the traditional village is a compact social, cultural, and economic unit that is relatively isolated from similar units, and therefore a more powerful molder of people than other forms of social life.

In the village, relations between the community and the individual, as well as among individuals, are mediated mainly by families. This basic cell of the community is a tightly knit amalgam of human functions—procreation, education, farming, and socializing—that in urban conditions are split into separate, multiple roles, played by members of the family inside and outside its confines. In the village, every person is in the public eye almost permanently and is expected to be visible and understood. Privacy has a very limited place in these conditions. Human contacts and communications are direct, deeply needed and, by definition, informal. The fleeting, formal, polite but shallow contacts so characteristic of the towns are rare in the experience of a villager. Everyone knows everybody, not just in the village but in the small nearest marketplace. Villagers feel secure in their rather predictable, familiar network of relations, based on a foundation of values acquired in similar circumstances and shared by their neighbors. Tradition, morality, work, and nature as well as established principles of a communal order all contribute to a way of life characterized by patriarchal authoritarianism and reliance on practice rather than abstractions. A syncretic correlation of the main social, cultural, and psychological features makes the mir—the village as a community and a "world"—into an "organic," as some say, or compact entity that has been able for centuries to resist endless pressures.

The small social world and its human relations are transparent and are perceived empirically, directly and sensually; whatever is less understandable or bewildering is handled by the magico-religious substratum of rural culture and psyche, where abstractions too are "ruralized," translated into practices and symbols familiar to the villagers and growing out of their needs and experience.

When "products" of this kind of socialization—even if their ethos is diluted considerably by economic development and urban influences—emigrate to towns, in particular if they have not had much urban experience, they face a world so different that their own is threatened with a precipitous and painful disintegration. Unless they can summon some resources of their small world, the migrants face a severe crisis of personality and moral values.

Tenacity of the rural spirit, nevertheless, is not always a stalwart defense against the disturbing effects of an often hostile new environment, so different from the familiar rural ways. A sense of loss, dissolution of moral certainties and criteria, and value crises often do occur—and on a large scale at that. In the context of the Soviet drive for overarching national objectives and the concomitant neglect of the microworlds, of privacy, and of the amenities and standards of living, a shattered or lost system of values and principles cannot easily and quickly be replaced by anything firm and wholesome. This problem is particularly acute in those newly burgeoning cities that themselves still lack solid cultural and institutional foundations.

When such phenomena are reproduced massively over an entire national system that is undergoing a hectic industrialization and urbanization, we can certainly speak of a stage, transitional, specific, and exhibiting complexities and aberrations in society, culture, and politics.

That is what we observe throughout Russian history, in different forms, but occurring with particular intensity in the 1930s and again after World War II. Nowadays ruralization on any significant scale cannot happen anymore, but the sequels of the previous stages and of the last, equally traumatic one are still part of the new urban scene.

The making of a stable and more self-controlling urban culture and moral world is certainly a difficult task. Once the aftershocks of the previous shattering events begin to subside, the cities begin to reconsider their own identities, and urban problems come to the fore, becoming the subject of public awareness and of political and scholarly treatment. But some of the older tasks remain on the agenda; the diminishing but still important battle between the rural and urban worlds, or cultures, continues. This is certainly a universal phenomenon in our time in urban societies in recently urbanized countries. In the Soviet case, an awareness of this phenomenon will help us to understand better some of the ambiguities we encounter when trying to interpret current events or gauge the prospects of current policies.

Having disposed, for the time being, of the rural impact on cities, we may now concentrate on the cities as urban objects per se. In countries still in the early stages of urbanization, the city tends to be viewed in comparison with the prevailing rural surrounding; the city is defined as a non-village. But with the unfolding of urbanization, the city emerges as a social reality whose particular dynamism cannot be grasped by any simple contrast with the rural world. The difficulty of defining the city, the urban phenomenon, is considerable, for a city is such a condensation of all kinds of dimensions and relations, of cultural trends, of professional and social differentiations, of sociopsychological and personality correlations. To isolate the essential qualities of the modern city, to define it, seems an incalculable task. One may be tempted to propose that the very complex condensation of innumerable traits in a limited space *is* the definition of a city. But it turns out that a defined and limited space is no longer a central trait. The modern ag-

glomeration belies any effort to define the urban phenomenon by reference to a single, easily identifiable
specimen, the city. Rather, we have to look at an intercity
system, a whole hierarchy of forms, a network of complicated interconnections on a national, even international scale.

Though such reflections belong in specialized treat-
ments of urban studies, without some sense of this modern concept of the city one cannot truly appreciate the
new reality that has emerged in the Soviet Union during
the past fateful three decades. I will have more to say
later about the effects of the *newness* of this structure—
the lingering peasant mentality and ancient mores being
one of its sequels—having to interact with traits of advanced urban society and culture. Sometimes it offers
the worst of both worlds, as the crude and uncouth
mores of disgruntled peasant-migrants bump up against
the seedier trends of advanced urban societies, such as
falling birth rates, gentrification, high rates of crime,
and widespread psychic stress. And it is not simply a
matter of dozens of individual cities undergoing urbanization. From the urban phenomenon in its fullness
emerges a hierarchical system that exhibits a great variety of forms and specific problems, replete with different cultural features, standards of living, and new ine-
qualities of status, culture, and national roles.

The varieties of towns and cities in Russia are not unlike those known elsewhere. Functionally, there are predominantly industrial, administrative, cultural, even
scientific cities, some of them subsisting on just one
branch of industrial activity or transportation. At the
other pole are the most developed, multifunctional centers, notably the capitals, mighty concentrations of eco-

nomic, political, and intellectual power. Population and propinquity also serve as classifying criteria. There are small, medium, large, very large, and megacities, some incorporated into a regional conurbation or agglomeration with easy intercity contact, others isolated in the Kazakh or Siberian wilderness. The problems created by this variety of forms are endless: contemporary Soviet studies give us ever more insight into the city system, its woes and prospects, policies already applied and new ones attempted. But the cry from many experts is for a program of integrated urban-rural development in order to master the huge country, punctuate it more uniformly with urban centers and conglomerates, resettle the population more evenly in and around powerful economic and cultural centers.

Music of the future? However grandiose the designs, they start from an ever more solid mastery of basic facts and phenomena, and it is rather the weight of those that can be read from the hopes pinned on the national programs for regulating urban development.

In the meantime, the plight of the small, rather isolated cities, crying out for revitalization, is also on the agenda. Many have been helped by an implantation of industry or assignment for a service function of importance (vacation spot, communication hub). Other small cities are decaying, losing their young people to the metropolises. Clearly, urbanization is not just the movement of people from the countryside to the city but from the small cities to the megacities.

It is this broad picture of social change induced by the spread and growth of cities, in particular of the large and largest ones, that sets the tone for the rest of the country, that in many ways actually defines the country today. Of course, other countries have had similar experiences, but not on such a scale, not so powerfully compressed in such a short period of time. And this in a country already a superpower even before urbanization was consummated.

For Russia, for the Soviet system, in any case, it is all new and unique.

3

Urban Society,
a New Labor Force

In the history of Soviet cities, we may single out three large waves of growth: the recovery of the urban population in the 1920s to the prerevolutionary levels, the feverish development during the 1930s, and the postwar boom, especially the period after 1956, when the bulk of the nation became urban.

The social consequences of this transformation unfolded in fits and starts and, quite naturally, the emergence of an urban social structure also came in stages and, as it were, in patches. New urban groups and forms appeared, including those considered as the most advanced in any given historical period, but then they took quite a time to prevail over older, simpler, or more primitive forms to which majorities of the population still belonged. Characteristic of any such transition are situations in which modes of life expressing an earlier social setting coexist with new ones that are to become tomorrow's prevailing reality.

As is well known, in their earlier stage most Russian

cities were quite rural. During the 1920s, in the very heart of Moscow, observers found, with disbelief, authentic villages over big areas of the capital. A recent review of Walter Benjamin's *Moscow Diary*, a log of his travels in Russia in 1925–1927, quotes Benjamin as saying that in the streets of Moscow "the Russian village plays hide-and-seek" [74:28]. Smaller cities were even more deeply villagelike, with country-style courtyards, thatched roofs, and in-court wells. As I mentioned earlier, the *byt*, the rural way of life, permeated these fledgling cities. In brief, these cities corresponded to a preindustrial stage in the social history of the country.

The next stage may be called, though without any claim to precision, the early industrial period, characterized by the prevalence, in the composition of the labor force, of simple physical labor, with low skills and relatively little use of advanced machinery. Even if the rural dwellings and gardens disappeared, they were replaced only by drab and monotonous rows of overcrowded and poorly serviced dwellings that housed this rather unskilled or primarily semiskilled labor. Similar developments had marked the earlier history of Western industrial cities, but in Russia this stage of industrialization evolved and continued, in part, into the current period; it was particularly characteristic of the pre- and postwar decades. In 1939, for example, 82.5 percent of the Soviet labor force was engaged in primarily physical labor, the remaining 17.5 percent in primarily intellectual work. Astonishingly, and very significantly, by 1959 the relative sizes of these sectors changed only slightly, to 79.3 percent and 20.7 percent [35:130].

Certainly this small shift represented a considerable number of workers. Yet "intellectual labor" (*umstvennyi trud*) is much too pompous a label for the professional reality of the Khrushchev era. Even in the cities, where by 1959 an apparently impressive 29.4 percent of the workforce was employed in the "intellectual" sector (compared to 57 percent in physical labor), the majority of these employees were plain, low-key nonspecialists, as the sociologists call them; in other words, rather primitive paper shufflers [90:247]. Which is to say that less than half of the so-called intellectual urban workforce was engaged in professional endeavors. And of this group, only some had any professional education. Many others, lacking formal education, learned on the job to be engineers and managers. This class of praktiki will be of some interest to us. They, too, symbolize an era.

A similarly low level of skill pervaded the manual labor force during this phase of Soviet industrialization. In most of the cities the composition of the manual labor force reflected the national priority to industrialize. In 222 of the 304 cities whose populations exceeded 50,000, a high proportion of the labor force—between 50 and 70 percent—was engaged in industry, transportation, and construction. In addition to the predominantly industrial cities, a considerable number, some 134 of the 304, can be characterized as diversified administrative centers. Harris, who cites these figures, observes that "the overwhelming predominance of these two types— namely the administrative and the industrial—reflects the nature of Soviet economy as a command economy where the political administration focused its attention primarily on the industrial side of the economy" [29:61].

Thus by 1959 the peasantry had been slowly replaced by a working class. However, initially, one type of predominantly physical labor was merely replacing another, although the new jobs were located in different and crucially important sectors. The earlier stages of this development deserve the epithet "extensive," as quantity and speed were the slogans of those years.

But during the next twenty years, we see the making of a more variegated and professionally differentiated national and urban social structure. Urbanization, industrial and scientifico-technical development, mass schooling and quality schooling, communications and arts, state policies and myriad spontaneous events changed the nation's overall social, professional, and cultural profile, and the social structure underwent a significant qualitative transformation. Workers in the national economy soared from about 24 million before the war, to almost 81 million in 1983; of these, the number engaged in industry jumped from 11 million to over 31 million. Transportation, construction, and communications also grew at a rapid pace; much more modest growth of employment was registered in different services. The role of the working class in the economy is underscored by the fact that it is now the prevailing group in society and in the cities: 61.5 percent of the population, almost twice their share in 1939. In comparison, the kolkhoz peasants, once over half of the population, are now barely 12.5 percent of the nation.

A second group, presented in Soviet statistics as "employees," increased from 11 million in 1941 to about 35 million in 1983, a rate of growth surpassing that of workers. To understand the importance of this group, we must turn to another way of classifying them.

"Specialists"—otherwise also called in the Soviet literature "intelligentsia"—show an even faster rate of growth than the category of "officials." Most notably, in 1941 only about 2.4 million of the 11 million employees had higher or specialized technical education; in 1960 only half of the 16 million employees were "specialists";

today, an overwhelming majority of officials accede to this category, thanks to considerably improved standards of professional education. Recent figures show over 31.5 million specialists, among them 13.5 million with higher education and over 18 million with specialized secondary training [70:397–99; 82:14].*

Before we turn to those officials *qua* "intelligentsia," let us survey the educational standards of the whole population. In 1939 the overwhelming majority of the workers and peasants had only an elementary education (four years of primary school). By 1959, little had changed: 91.3 percent of workers and 98.2 percent of kolkhoz peasants still achieved only elementary standards. But by 1984 no more than 18.5 percent of manual laborers had only an elementary education—and, one would assume, a majority of the least educated were from the older generation [99:18–19].

In the population at large the massive educational efforts yielded significant results. Forty-six million people received a "secondary incomplete" education (seven years of schooling). Fifty-eight million enjoyed a full secondary education, which is now legally obligatory for all children. Alumni of the "secondary specialized" establishments that train technicians of all denominations numbered 28 million. A full higher education was received by 18.5 million people, and another 3.6 million received an incomplete higher education.

Among university and high school graduates, the numbers of men and women are substantially equal. Women constitute 54 percent of university students, 58

*Since the major trends, and not the precise demographic statistics, are of most concern in this interpretive sketch, all the figures presented here have been rounded off. For the exact data, readers should consult the sources cited in the text.

percent of the enrollment in secondary specialized schools, and 60 percent of all specialists with both higher and secondary education. Further, though women constitute 51 percent of the labor force as a whole, they account for about 56 percent of educated specialists, and 40 percent of scientists and scholars [99:7]. This emancipation of women—for centuries the predominantly uneducated mass and the most neglected—is perhaps the most visible part of what can be called the Soviet "cultural revolution." (This term was improperly applied by official propaganda to the 1930s, when most citizens received barely three to four years of elementary education. Today, millions attend universities and high schools, and all children have access to at least a modicum of instruction. But by now, of course, "cultural revolution" acquires a new meaning again.)

Thus the development of professional and educational standards that began in the 1930s only to be interrupted by the ordeal of World War II, has come to fruition on a large scale during the last three decades. In particular, we must emphasize the making and remaking of the Soviet intelligentsia.*

The history of the intelligentsia is tortuous, even tortured, but it has now become, in fact, a mass of people, composed of all the professionals the modern world re-

---

*Soviet authors argue whether technicians with secondary special education should be included in the intelligentsia, a term that implies not only high professional skill but also an appropriate cultural background and the ability to use—if not create—concepts. Although this argument is of interest, it can be disregarded here. My primary point is that the creation of a layer of professionally and intellectually advanced people has long been at the center of Russian and Soviet theoretical and ideological debates. The Soviet leadership has always dreamed of producing a broad layer of such people, who would emerge from the popular classes and become committed to the new regime.

quires and of numerous groups, subgroups, and categories: technical, managerial-administrative, scientific, artistic, educational, and political. Even if we restrict ourselves to those with a higher education, their number reaches now about 15 million, a vast pool of "grey matter" and the fastest-growing part of the new social structure. While the employed population grew by 155 percent between 1960 and 1986, the number of specialists grew fourfold. Over 5 million students are attending institutions of higher education, taught by half a million professors [31:65].

An even slightly more rapid growth has occurred in the sector of scientific and technological research. Scientists and engineers working in research today number almost 1.5 million, flanked by a large cadre of auxiliary technicians—a serious and sizable "branch of the national economy," as a Soviet scholar termed it [87:110–11].

We will not at this point enter into the problems faced by these groups and classes—the imbalances, inefficiencies and general shortfalls that have resulted, notably, from their hectic formation. Whatever the problems, ailments, and even crises, they reflect a qualitatively different social structure than that of fifty years ago. In effect, in the past five decades the USSR has leaped into the twentieth century, although in the 1930s most of the nations of the territory still belonged to a far earlier age. The creation of the techno-scientific and intellectual class, accompanying the urbanization process, is thus a momentous development. The further advance of the economy and the survival of the political system are dependent on this layer, which has become a large, almost "popular" mass.

I will later explore the political sequels of these phenomena, but some implications are obvious already. The new intelligentsia, members of the different categories of this stratum, have moved beyond research institutes and universities. Numbers of them are government experts, medium- and top-level executives, participants and members of the highest administrative and political apparaty. And it is a sign of the new times in Russia that this amalgam is deepening and expanding. Studying this stratum, which supplies "cadres"—we may also say "elites"—for the system, will help us to understand the future of Russia and how it will meet the next century.

———

In the USSR today, the professional classes and the intellectuals direct all spheres of economic, political, and social life. (They did so even in conditions in which their own personal freedoms were denied to them.) Nevertheless, they are dependent on an important layer of less-qualified but vitally important "technicians," most of whom are trained in the system of "specialized secondary education." Without these technicians, the high-ranking specialists are incapacitated—as is quite well known to any student of the Soviet industrial and scientific establishments. Unfortunately, an impetuous cadres policy has pressed for ever more high-level specialists and neglected the formation of middle-rank technicians; the whole system was severely handicapped by the resulting imbalances. A similar situation developed in other sectors and lower layers in the productive and social ladder. Medium- and high-ranking specialists simply cannot operate efficiently unless they have enough skilled and motivated paraprofessionals and assistants.

It is obvious that the nation's entire workforce is an

interconnected system vulnerable to professional and social impairment if it is not continuously readjusted and re-equilibrated. Structural imbalances of different types have always plagued the Soviet economy, and this vexed problem is again on the agenda in a grand way.

The nationwide restructuring of the urban socio-professional profile described earlier in this chapter resulted from a historical process of readjustment that was only in part affected by policies. Short-term measures, after all, have little impact on massive social changes. Indeed, the government's day-to-day tinkering with the professional structure may even make things worse. Longer-term policies are indispensable at this stage, as they were during the upheavals in the 1930s, to provide coordinated measures in the educational and administrative areas, in labor and wage policies, and in the general realm of motivation and incentives.

As a result of the broad historical processes and direct interventions of policy, today's employed urban population falls into three groups: almost 60 percent are workers, about 40 percent are officials and specialists, and some 1 to 5 percent are kolkhoz peasants, most of whom live in the smaller towns and work in nearby kolkhozy.

Let us examine the first two groups more closely. Of the workers, 10–12 percent are unskilled or poorly skilled; 44–46 percent are skilled physical workers, the backbone of the industrial labor force; and 3–4 percent are highly skilled workers whose duties are deemed to require physical and intellectual aptitudes [92:23]. Much fuss was made by apologists who saw this highest layer as boding a future merger of intellectual and physical labor and the disappearance of all social inequality and classes. In fact, the thinness of this layer points to the rather poor state of the current industrial organization, still underequipped in advanced mechanisms and automation. Nevertheless, considering that youth now coming into the factories are rather well educated, they may be ready to learn high-level skills, if the new equipment does appear. Here is a faint hint of yet another important imbalance and social problem: too many well-educated people and not enough challenging, demanding jobs.

In the officials-cum-specialists group, 11–12 percent are poorly trained or untrained; 17–18 percent are in professional jobs demanding good training in secondary and specialized schools or in universities; 2.5–3 percent are in medium-rank managerial and professional positions that demand university schooling and additional training; and the top 2 percent perform highly skilled, largely intellectual functions in upper-rank leadership positions.

From these figures, it is quite easy to see the historical leap, in comparison with the NEP or any later stage, in the restructuring of the national labor force. But it is difficult to assess whether this is an adequate professional structure for the new age and what its dynamics are. A more fruitful approach has been proposed by two able Soviet sociologists, L. A. Gordon and V. V. Komarovskii [23:98–110]. In order to analyze the role of the professional structure in the development of the socioeconomic system, they studied three generations in the active working population: men born around 1910, who entered the labor force in the 1930s and reached their vocational peak in the 1950s; their sons, born in the 1930s, who entered the labor force in the 1950s and peaked in the 1970s; and their grandsons, born in the 1950s, who entered the labor force in the 1970s.

The vocational x-ray of these three generations, which now coexist and often work together, confirms and highlights the findings we have already reached from other sources and data on Soviet social development. Generation by generation, fewer people are working in agriculture and at physical labor; more people are employed in nonmanual jobs in industry, services, and information.* But this generational approach also vividly suggests the interactions and clashes that characterized the historical change of the guard.

The first generation carried the nation through the period of industrialization but was nevertheless predominantly employed in jobs that did not demand much if any schooling. These men were physical laborers of the traditional type, almost preindustrial in character, and many were still peasants. Even at the height of their careers, in the 1950s, 80 percent of them continued to do physical labor.

In the second generation, we see some results of the nation's industrialization. This generation was the first in which more workers were employed in industry than in agriculture; the first in which skilled labor predominated over unskilled physical labor; and the first in which the number of nonmanual workers equaled that of unskilled manual workers. But alongside the important shift from agriculture to industry and the lower ra-

*Gordon and Komarovskii have not yet published a complete set of data. Their preliminary analyses show that the percentage of the labor force employed in unskilled physical labor has decreased from 50 percent (cohort 1) to 29 percent (cohort 2) to 17 percent (cohort 3). Regarding field of employment: the percentage of workers involved in agriculture has dropped from 40 percent (cohort 1) to 22 percent (cohort 2) to 13 percent (cohort 3); the percentage employed in industry has increased from 38 percent (cohort 1) to 48 percent (cohort 2) to 50 percent (cohort 3).

tio of unskilled workers, this cohort's advance into the branches of information, services, and organization was modest.

In the third generation we see a substantial increase in the numbers engaged in the service and information professions, and a corresponding decrease in unskilled manual laborers and agriculturists. From the very start of their careers, twice as many of this cohort are entering the intellectual labor force as the physical labor force. Herein we see the industrial era yielding to the scientific-industrial-information era. Already this youngest generation lives in a different environment and faces different pressures.

Gordon and Komarovskii calculate that in contemporary society one-fourth of each generation moves up the socioprofessional ladder, and they predict that vocational mobility will probably accelerate. Unfortunately, these authors do not indicate whether this rate of intergenerational mobility is sufficient, nor do they cite the relevant Western figures for comparison. But, as they note, this rate is high enough to create tensions among the generations. The young quickly develop different styles of life, form new approaches to life and work, and often reject, we can safely add, the methods and culture of their predecessors.

Such tensions are unavoidable and not unexpected, and they are likely to increase in the coming decade as intragenerational changes accelerate. In the 1990s, Gordon and Komarovskii project, the proportion of crude agricultural and industrial labor will drop to barely 10 percent among the third generation, as it approaches its career peak, and close to 40 percent of this cohort will be employed in intellectual professions. And the researchers predict that 30–40 percent of the workforce will be involved in sociocultural and other services and in professions related to the creation and processing of information. These projections lag behind current Western professional profiles: In the West more people are already engaged in information and services, fewer in industry, and very few in agriculture. But the authors do not seem unduly worried, for the lag, they observe, can be addressed by informed government policies. (The researchers are probably quite sincere. The best of contemporary social science in the Soviet Union is no longer content to issue soothing and reassuring prognoses, as was expected of them by the older-style leaders. Today, a growing number of scholars seeks to expose the sharper and more menacing aspects of social life; they issue warnings and demand action.)

Yet Gordon and Komarovskii caution that this inter- and intragenerational thrust forward into modern intellectual and professional life portends social trouble of great magnitude if it is not matched by reforms in the prevailing economic mechanism and in the "relations of production" [23:108–10]. The different spheres of the socioeconomic system suffer from discordances (*rassoglasovanie*) that threaten the nation's entire professional and educational endeavor. The state cannot allow "a socioprofessional structure adequate to the needs of a scientific-industrial system to be straitjacketed into a production system that is still stuck in an earlier technical and technological age." In the absence of reform, not only will professionalization not improve the performance of the system, it could also create widespread social crises and even pressures to return to the old patterns.

The stern warning sounded by these researchers may seem overly alarmist, but it reflects recent developments well known to readers of Soviet sociology. The list is long: widespread job dissatisfaction among educated youth and highly trained professionals; low morale— poor "sociopsychological climate" is the Soviet term— in many workplaces; underutilized engineers and scientists who waste their time on menial jobs because of a shortage of technicians and auxiliary personnel; hordes of poorly trained people parading, easily, as engineers or scientists. These images of a wasted generation and a potentially disastrous backsliding for the whole country certainly hang over the heads of the nation's political and economic leadership.

"Caveant consules!" the scholars caution. But these days they seem to believe that the consuls, or some of them, are aware.

4

The Intelligentsia

Among the sociological and cultural changes of the post-Stalinist period, we earlier singled out the transformation of the professional layer of specialists into a mass phenomenon. The increasing number of professionals working in research and development, in communications, and in the arts signals the remaking and reemergence of stable, massive professional and cultural classes—a vast pool from which new leaders and elites are arising. Most importantly, the different approaches, outlooks, and ideologies that prevail among and within the generations are coexisting and competing without destroying each other.

This latter point is, of course, a novelty in Soviet history, where one destructive period followed another; repeatedly, the best cadres in the nation were decimated, and incumbent and potential leaders in politics, society, and culture were slaughtered. These chapters of Soviet history are well known, but it is worth recalling that the story of "elites" has been complicated from the moment the Russian Revolution occurred because of the paucity of adequate cadres or their unreliability, real or presumed, from the standpoint of the new regime's security and aims. The story of those groups that ruled the country is still to be written, but some stages can be sketched out briefly, both to intimate the problems and also to buttress my central interpretive arguments.

Indisputably, the revolution and the civil war inflicted considerable losses on the country's professional classes. Many died, others fled abroad, and many of the survivors who remained were either distrustful or distrusted. Nevertheless, pragmatism prevailed: the system could not function without these specialists. The politico-administrative elite, the groups in the upper echelons of government, came to be composed of a curious mélange of ex-professional revolutionaries, many poorly trained but politically reliable cadres from worker and peasant stock, and a crucial admixture of specialists called "bourgeois" because they were trained and privileged in the previous regime.

Mistrust and complicated love-hate relations were common in the government, and to some extent, although on different grounds, in the party. But it was the "bourgeois" group that constituted the class of experts who helped build the government machinery during the 1920s. (Some had already helped the Soviets earlier, notably in the Red Army.)

This explosive alliance was disturbed in the late twenties by the persecution of the ex-tsarist experts. These attacks subsided by 1932, but by then the institutions and the economy had so greatly expanded that the small numbers of the "ex-bourgeois" became a drop—though important because of their quality—in the sea of newcomers from the ranks and from the institutions of higher education.

All the institutions churning out the neophyte cadres were still in their infancy, but they hurried to produce the graduates badly needed by the expanding nonagricultural sector. From the midst of these newcomers, most of whom were from popular classes, were now selected in growing numbers the emerging elites. Concomitantly, the numbers of ex-revolutionaries (not just old Bolsheviks) and members of the prerevolutionary intelligentsia (several tens of thousands of "bourgeois" specialists at the end of the NEP) dwindled quite rapidly.

Among the newcomers, the category of praktiki was particularly numerous. Since the schools were not yet capable of satisfying the voracious demand for cadres, many people with no formal preparation received all their professional training on the job. Even those who benefitted from some preparation were most often inadequately trained. Such educational deficiencies were common in all walks of life, especially in the sphere of politics. Most of the political cadres had less education than other professions; they were trained or trained themselves on the job as best they could [62:38–41].

For a short time, some progress in schooling cadres was made. But the subsequent Stalinist purges severely obstructed the emergence and improvement of the professional and cultural classes. Countless up-and-coming professionals were murdered, and the asphyxiating atmosphere of the Stalinist counterrevolution stifled the flow of advanced and sophisticated ideas.

The damage to the nation's political and professional upper layers was enormous. The costly efforts of producing adequate leadership were wasted by a mass slaughter, notably of old Bolsheviks and of many Stalinists. The new replacements were often of lesser cultural and especially political standards and, of course, had less, if any, experience compared to those who had been purged. Further, this newest layer of elites was the third in a short period of time. A general deterioration of the country's political culture, including a decline in the top political echelons, ensued. By the end of Stalin's rule, and for some time thereafter, both the highest echelons and the political system at large were beset by an acute crisis of values and of leadership. A blind wall stood between the rulers and the ruled.

In the late 1950s and early 1960s, Khrushchev's efforts to open up and reform the system met with some success. But his initiatives were often frustrated by the growing complexity of problems, by the immense scale of social change, and by the limitations of a political system that provided for the handling of basic needs but did not promote any broader strategies for more substantive change. Still, the sum of small improvements—and a few spectacular ones—was far from negligible. The battered and much maligned bureaucracy had become more stable and potent, and it succeeded in imposing on the system a more acceptable and, from the bureaucracy's point of view, a far more secure and more professional method of ruling. More attention to the laws, better control of the police, elimination of the Stalinist concentration camps, the implementation of group or "collective" leadership: the list of improvements is impressive. For the first time, a consolidated ruling apparatus exercised control over the whole of the state machinery, and the stabilization and security thereby offered to functionaries resulted in many of the improvements that the citizens of the USSR experienced up through the late sixties.

But in the following two decades, the elite and the medium and lower layers in government began to lose momentum and to lose touch. The development of the country outraced the governing abilities of the networks in power. *Rassoglasovannost'*, discordances and imbalances, spread throughout the system, widening the chasm between the mentality and professional abilities of top and medium-ranking cadres and the new realities of the day.

Was there during the 1970s and early 1980s enough renovation within the system to prepare a change of guard, whether the older generation wanted it or not? Was there some open or subterranean influx of new cadres in the bureaucracies and the networks close to them?

We know that changes were taking place on an intergenerational level in the working population at large. Something was going on in the party and state, too—though we have less material about them, except for data on the improved educational standards of most cadres. Too, it is unmistakably clear that the praktiki were disappearing. At the end of 1956, 57.2 percent of all industrial specialists of the USSR were still praktiki. Unbelievable as it may sound for a country that was already a superpower, 68.4 percent of factory directors, even 32.9 percent of all chief engineers and technical directors, belonged to this category. By the mid-sixties the proportions of praktiki had fallen substantially, and today the phenomenon is largely vestigial. Parallel developments have taken place in the political *apparaty*, with those at the very top being more resilient to the call of changing times than the layers just below them.

Further evidence of a partial modernization in the top cadres and their outlook comes from a study [61] of the efforts deployed by a group of leaders to reform the economy in the mid-sixties. An alliance of experts, managers, top government officials, and some party leaders fought tooth and nail for the preferred changes. Their main promoter was Prime Minister Kosygin, and with his support some battles were won. The reforms were launched, but were blocked by a coalition of conservatives and hardline ideologues. The infighting and internal struggles of those years seem to prefigure the even broader alliances that are battling it out today.

5

The Urban Microworlds and Their Power

One of the effects of massive urbanization was the increased visibility of problems that were once disregarded, swept under the carpet, because of the state's other preponderant interests. We have in mind, on the one hand, the intricate world and interests of the person or individual (*lichnost'* in Soviet terminology) and, on the other, the multitude of small-scale, primary social forms that sustain individuals in their everyday life, that support their moral equilibrium and psychic health—or, as the case may be, undermine them.

The incredible social and psychological maze that is the city compelled scholars—in the footsteps of urban professionals who address everyday social problems (social workers, teachers, policemen, doctors)—to delve into the small-scale forms of everyday life. Previously, most of the political and hence also scholarly attention was focused on the macrodimensions—economic development, broadly defined social classes, national systems of education—and there was a tendency to believe that changes in the large-scale systems would force all the small-scale forms to follow suit.

There is not much left of this naive fascination with the primacy of the large-scale and massive dimensions of social life. Besides the inescapable countertrend that views the personal, intimate, and small-scale as the sole worthwhile dimension of life, Soviet scholars, leaders, and pedagogues have come to focus more closely on human relations, whatever their scale, and their interrelations and relatively independent momentums. In both the academic and political communities, the entire gamut of social forms of life has assumed a crucial importance for even the most broadly viewed objectives of national politics.

Hence a proliferation of discussions and research, and a broad preoccupation with subjects long familiar in the West but novel in the USSR. Moreover, these social analyses are now perceived as having deep implications for the political sphere. Themes like personality, individuality, and personal autonomy and issues of how to create an environment that enriches personal life have become important not just in scholarly circles, where such subjects have been debated in serious texts for more than a decade, but also in political discourse, which certainly borrowed from the scholarly literature. Undoubtedly, this emphasis on personal life is one of the results of Soviet urbanization. Freedom of movement, choice of profession, multiple choices in many walks of life—such rights are being demanded by the new waves of better-educated and more intellectual urban professionals.

That the city, more than any other environment, provokes critical faculties and intellectual freedom is, of course, a textbook truism. But despite the theoretical commonplaceness of it all, when an authoritarian social system begins to rediscover such terms and phenomena, we are witnessing an important event. For more than a decade at least one Soviet scholar, O. N. Ianitskii, has published articles on the theme that "the development of man as an individual and as a productive force becomes the center of gravity in the formation of modern cities" [34:38]. Over time, many others developed similar ideas until, finally, the party leader took it up as a key direction of policy. Such a turnabout is not just *in posse*; it must already be, to some extent, *in esse*. Ianitskii adds an example that will help us understand how urbanization manifests its social essence. As numerous studies of workers' preferences and behavior have shown, and Ianitskii cites some of the most important ones, most workers are equally sensitive to both the natural and social conditions of life: "Particularly substantive is the propensity to an integrative, syncretic understanding by people of their life conditions—they are not satisfied anymore with some set or other of specific conditions, they demand a new quality of the whole life environment." This is the type of issue confronting the politicians to whom the article is addressed.

The personal dimension also assumes a new importance in the contemporary techno-scientific revolution, which so intensifies the density of human communications in urban life. As Ianitskii puts it, "The advance of the scientific-technological revolution and of urbanization are intimately connected with the principle of autonomous activity of the person, of contacts between individuals as individuals" [32:74]. And here, again, he offers a directly political conclusion: such communications, which are the very condition of creativity, cannot exist in a coercive environment. Other Soviet scholars studying scientific activities have repeated the same thesis in different forms. Scholarship demands freedom of the individual scholar, who is the best carrier of ideas that fuel scientific advances. The role of free exchanges is often illustrated by the importance of the "invisible college," one type of informal group specific to the scholarly community.

This argument has implications that transcend the academic world. Demands concerning freedoms for scholars reverberate on a broader scale and are presented as a universal need and right. The theme of *prava lichnosti*, "the rights of the individual," has already attracted quite a literature, and today it does not sound like just another empty word. Scholars and political essayists are quite categorical: the continuing denial of indispensable rights will precipitate devastating results. Officials are again duly forewarned that appeals for economic intensification and high productivity will only provoke another fiasco if the issues of rights are not addressed.

So much for personality and individuality per se. Before moving on to the welter of informal groups, we must mention, however briefly, one small but rather formal group: the family. Not surprisingly, the family has also been studied as one of the roots of the autonomous individual. One scholar emphasizes that the modern urban family, whatever its problems, is characterized by a higher degree of personal autonomy for all its members, including women, youths, and even small children [78:97]. Families promote the growing quest for and use of individual autonomy and help spread it through the population at large with an irresistible power, and this process is autonomous, that is, spontaneous. Among 70 million Soviet families, one can be sure that many millions encourage an irresistible molecular pressure for autonomy and, we should add, privacy. Although the latter concept is not yet used directly, it is implied in the demands for *prava lichnosti, uvelichenie lichnoi avtonomii* ("rights and increased autonomy of individuals") and in the effort to strengthen the role of the family as a socializing force in society. Though some observers claim that in modern life the socializing role of the family has irretrievably yielded to large-scale forces like schooling, the media, and politics, most sociologists and other professionals involved propose the opposite conclusion. For them it is not the family that is an auxiliary of the state in socializing youth, but rather the other way around. Empirical studies show that when asked about the importance of different factors in their education, most respondents named the family as the most influential. The authors of one such study conclude that "social institutions and social organizations are only assisting the family, but cannot replace it" [92:87].

That the family is part of a system and adapts to changes in that system is a foregone conclusion. But the family has very specific functions and is endowed with its own impetus and an autonomy of sorts. Recognizing the dangers and futility of excessive regulation, contemporary Soviet legislation regulates the family only minimally, except to safeguard the rights of its members.

But the autonomous character of the family, its strengths and weaknesses, are also fashioned by heritage, tradition, and convention. For one group of authors "the most important regulator of human behavior in family life is a historically formed system of sociocultural and ethnocultural norms, which includes both norms formed in the past and those that emerge in contemporary conditions" [92:88]. This historical influence is best illustrated by regional or ethnic cultural and behavior patterns.

There are in the USSR, broadly, two patterns of "demographic conduct"—a problem of immense importance in view of the decline of birthrates in the cities. One pattern, which is widespread in the European part of the USSR, is based on individual decisions, relatively independent of any group norms, in questions concerning procreation; having children is a choice guided by very personal motivations and aims. The other pattern, which predominates in Central Asia, still follows the traditional norms, which disregard individual aims and instil a particular way of life [92:89].

A recent article by a noted student of the Soviet family, A. G. Kharchev [45], paints a very troubling picture of family problems, especially in the big cities: Youth are poorly prepared for marriage and their marital relations are relatively fragile; sexual exploitation, moral turpitude, and extramarital pregnancies seem to be on the rise; and too many children live in families without fathers. These problems are not unusual, of course, to observers of Western societies. Kharchev, however, raises one problem that is more common in the Soviet way of thinking than in the West. The education system, he claims, is busy spreading some forms of knowledge, but it does not educate the young, for knowledge in itself cannot establish an ethos or cultural values (*kulturnost'*), and principles that guide people's behavior. The chasm in Soviet society between the standards of educational achievement and the more profound spiritual culture of society is exemplified by the disparity between "higher socialist values" and behavior in the sphere of marital relations [45:31].

These themes have direct repercussions in the realm of politics, as political discourse responds to the realization that social reality, notably its small forms, is a power not at all small. Despite the statist setting, social microforms have their own impetus and participate in creating and recreating the spiritual and moral world of the citizenry. These microforms can be gravely damaged by too crude an administrative interference in the sphere of the personal and the familial, in neighborly relations, friendly groups, and other informal structures. Criminal behavior, of course, demands government intervention, but overzealousness in regulating the microforms in general may contribute to an increase in the less palatable phenomena.

It goes without saying that such theorems shatter the older stereotypes of bureaucratic thinking, which is premised on the primacy of state and politics in national life. Such a view of politics must be scrapped when events force politicians to learn about all kinds of informal structures—including those inside the bureaucracies (which they certainly knew about from experience but didn't want to acknowledge) and the invisible college of scholars—and their role in shaping the individual, his motivations and behavior. Should politicians fail to understand this lesson and in some way weaken urban microforms they will create for the authorities new nightmares. For it is only with the help of informal groups—friends at work and in school, fellow-villagers—that millions of migrants manage the difficult process of adaptation to city life.

But more: sociological surveys of young migrant textile workers "allow [us] to state with some assurance that in the majority of cases, the most basic [social] relations are formed with comrades at work and in schools" [48:194]. (We notice that it is not the Komsomol, the official youth organization, that is of any importance here; it is not mentioned in any of these studies.) On a similar line, scholars studying mass communications and their effect on public opinion are reporting on the crucial role of the small groups. It turns out that whatever people read in the press or see on television undergoes a considerable "working over" (*obrabotka*). The impact of the media is controlled by the sometimes even more powerful influence of interpersonal communications within informal and small groups. The same happens, certainly, in all the professions, notably in professional informal groups of *intelligenty*, whose influence may be even stronger than that of workers' groups.

One survey, conducted in a factory in Leningrad, concerned the relative influence of television programs and discussions with friends on workers' opinions of ideological questions. While 24.5 percent of the respondents said that watching television does not change their opinions (we do not know whether they agreed or disagreed with the program), 58 percent stated that their opinions do change after discussions with friends, colleagues, and relatives. Another survey in a number of Leningrad factories reports that 98 percent of the respondents obtain their information from the media, 90 percent of those discuss what they learn with friends and family, and 42 percent modify their views after such discussions. The reasons most often given for such changes of heart were: "The authority of my interlocutor influenced me"; "I accepted the opinion of the group"; "They simply made me change my mind"; and "I received additional information" [78:105].

Official views espoused by the media are, in effect, filtered twice: by the small group's leader and by the small group as a whole [77:48]. Thus interpersonal contacts, if they have a relatively stable character based on common interests, can be more powerful forums of self-expression than any other form of communications, even media of "the most intense and massive character" [77:49].

In conclusion, the microenvironment serves as a relay between the mass media and the individual [92:20]. The Soviet mass media cannot out-and-out brainwash people because interpersonal contacts—the maze of relatives, informal groups, and other broader social entities—serve as a shield against at least the cruder forms of indoctrination. No wonder the departments of agitation and propaganda repeatedly discover that their mass propaganda is often quite ineffective, sometimes even entirely a waste. The microcosms of urbanized society can prove stronger than the political macrocosm if "the group" feels that the official spokesman is "talking empty."

6

Underpinnings of Public Opinion

We can now reexamine many of the social forms, especially the microstructures of urban society discussed or
alluded to in the preceding chapters, from a somewhat
different point of view. Earlier, our concern was with
the recognition that personal communications, and
their intensification in response to the growth and further differentiation of urban social structures, are an
indispensable precondition for creativity, problem solving, and proper social relations in cities. Such communications become human relations inside the different
small-scale forms of life—family, friends, localized
communities, a variety of nonformal contact groups—
that shelter individuals from the depersonalizing pro-
pensities of urban life by creating a counter balance for
the fleeting, shallow, and stressful multiplicity of roles
that cities impose on their residents. And, as we have
already learned, these social forms provide a filter and
corrective for the streams of information, images, and
propaganda that the mass media emit.

As we move up the ladder from interpersonal communications and nonformal microgroups, the next rung is a broader form of contacts that are intermediary between the microforms and the large-scale citywide, regional, and national formations. One example of these, mentioned in the previous chapter, is the "invisible college," a term used in Western sociology of science to denote the vital informal local, national, and international contacts among scholars in different disciplines. Such contacts outside the confines of the workplace are considered a sine qua non of scientific creativity. Labeled *nezrimye kollektivy uchenykh* in the USSR, invisible colleges have been extolled as a necessity of scholarly life that both personally benefits individual scholars and enhances the sociopsychological climate in their home institutions [77:21–22]. Absence of such contacts may deprive a scholar, even whole scholarly branches, of indispensable information and stimulation and cause them to lag behind international standards.

In different organizations—workshops, administrations, small and large bureaucracies—a similar but broader phenomenon has been fully recognized by contemporary Soviet scholars. The so-called "informal structures" supplement an organization's formal ones, sometimes creating a productive symbiosis [1:171–77]. But often, as is well known from Western studies, formal and informal are juxtaposed in an uneasy coexistence, which is not surprising, since informal structures represent correctives or straightforward defensive mechanisms against the tensions and imbalances that the formal structures fail to overcome. The informal structures may produce informal leaders or illicit practices, which the formal leadership must often tolerate, sometimes almost legitimize, so that the system can continue to work. Influential informal structures are also found in the larger social arena, for example, the force of public opinion.

Belatedly, Soviet political science, itself a recent, still fledgling apparition, has bowed to the evidence and acknowledged that "it is not possible to deny the existence of informal structures," which come into being because "the human factor manifests itself in management networks in different forms" [20:71]. Soviet sociologists, however, are much more advanced than their political science brethren and some time ago began to analyze the panoply or hierarchy of contact groups, especially the nonformal ones. The sociological literature presents substantial evidence that contact groups are an important component of Soviet public opinion and constitute an increasingly potent force in Soviet public and private life. In 1987 the world press learned about this power when the leadership publicly acknowledged the public's demand for discontinuing the project of deflecting the flow of Siberian rivers toward the southern dry lands. No longer can observers dismiss public opinion as but a minor factor in Soviet political life. Indeed, the recognition of public opinion is by now almost a new ideological official tenet, as we will shortly see.

Actually, the power of public opinion had already been demonstrated during Khrushchev's term, when his plan for educational reforms ran afoul of widespread opposition in influential layers of the population, causing the plan to be abandoned. Though this story was noticed by Western scholars of Soviet education and by some political scientists, no broader conclusions were drawn. Nonetheless, theoretical and empirical studies of public opinion and its mechanisms have been on the Soviet agenda for quite some time. Even one rather cautious earlier book, published in 1975 and still couched in conventional ideological terms, is quite unequivocal on some basic issues. Public opinion, the author's argument

runs [86], is an independent social phenomenon that—
we may infer, though the author does not say so explic-
itly—differs from the previously manipulated, so-called
obshchestvennost'.* Neither the party nor the trade
unions, which were officially considered the spokesmen
of public interest, can claim to truly represent public
opinion. On the contrary, these official groups cannot
perform their political role without fully recognizing,
studying, and responding to public opinion.

There is no doubt that such is in fact the case. We have
already seen how small groups correct and often coun-
teract the official media, and this same process applies
to many other tenets, including ideological ones.
Through persistent and confidential formal, semiformal,
and informal contacts, the formal and informal structures exchange information and opinions. Exchanges occur among workers and technicians, inside economic
and political administrations, and in offices, think tanks,
and institutes. Oral opinions, position papers, and various samizdats (many more, in fact, than those that
reached the West during a time when only extreme criticisms and disclosures were preferred) participate in informing and forming public opinion, in tandem or
against the official media, on social as well as political
problems of all kinds. That artistic productions—theatrical, cinematic, and, especially, literary—are both powerful shapers of public opinion as well as its spokesmen
is by now well known.

Even a quick perusal of the latest periodicals shows
the breadth of interest in the study of public opinion.

---

*A system by which the party named individuals, most of whom
were officials, to serve as formal representatives of society, ostensibly
independent of the government. These representatives' opinions were
sought mostly on foreign affairs, less frequently on domestic issues.

The quarterly of Moscow University, *Vestnik*, published a number of such studies in 1986. The popular sociological monthly *Sotsiologicheskie Issledovaniia* (Sociological Inquiries) studied "public opinion and its fight with drunkenness and alcoholism" (no. 1, 1986) and "public opinion on the situation in the workplace" [24]. And in the monthly of the Academy of Sciences, *Sovetskoe Gosudarstvo i Pravo* (Soviet State and Law), E. L. Bonk raised the topic of "sociological studies of public opinion about law" [8:120–23].

It is well worth our while to dwell for a moment on this last article, both for the opinions and the research findings Bonk quotes. Large-scale sociological surveys were conducted by the Institute for Interdisciplinary Social Studies of Leningrad University with the goal of constructing a scale of factors that influence people's choice of rightful behavioral patterns. The surveys reveal that public opinion plays an important role in decisions of different collectivities. In one survey, 63 percent of the respondents stated that they resolved real-life dilemmas on ethical grounds; only 21 percent let themselves be guided by their understanding of the law; the rest, presumably, followed what they considered to be public opinion. These results suggest a rather low degree of legal culture among the respondents and only a minimal role for public opinion. But a different picture emerged when a controlling question couched in broader terms was asked: What are your guiding criteria of behavior in complicated situations when an independent decision has to be made? Here 56 percent said they were guided by prevailing opinion in their collectivity, and only 7 percent mentioned the factor of existing laws.

Among state officials a somewhat different, but in substance analogous, situation obtained: 22 percent let themselves be guided by knowledge of the laws, 35 percent heed public opinion, 36 percent reflect upon politico-ethical aspects of the problem, and 65 percent gauge economic expediency (respondents were allowed to cite more than one criterion).

Bonk cautions his readers not to confound the concept of "legal consciousness"—opinions about the law, knowledge of the law—with "public opinion about the law." The latter, which is his chief concern, reflects a complicated composite of numerous factors that characterize the state of social consciousness at any given time; massive and relatively stable, it is guided predominantly not by juridical, but by moral and political criteria. Public opinion, he continues, is a powerful force insofar as it expresses far more than people's opinions. For at the root of public opinion are the social interests perceived by a group, or a whole nation. When deeply felt, these social interests and the opinions they engender command conduct and different forms of action. Therefore, public opinion is not just the opinion of a collectivity about some event or law, but also an expectation, a practical reaction that is not always restricted to official channels. Emotions have their part in public opinion, as does much that is erroneous or shortsighted.

As Bonk notes, public opinion does not react to everything that goes on, but selectively identifies important problems. The recent governmental action against drunkenness and alcoholism has elicited public support, he claims—but the indisputable implication is that such support may not always be forthcoming.

The phenomenon of public opinion has been part of Soviet life for some time already; studies, surveys, and polls are conducted relatively frequently; and today public opinion is a powerful agent in political affairs

But only recently has this phenomenon attracted attention in the West, and then only after General Secretary Gorbachev remarked in a well-publicized speech that the party recognizes public opinion and wants to work in concert with it. (The statement is of great importance, but might not commentators have noticed this development before the Soviet party leader told us to do so?)

Public opinion is, no doubt, the product of social mechanisms similar to those we have discussed in describing the smaller and intermediate urban social groups and currents. In the formation of public opinion, groups such as ethnic minorities, professional and cultural milieus, and a host of informal networks each play a part. As we have seen, public opinion, with or without official sanction, is a guide to personal action for many. But recently a broader phenomenon is commanding attention: unofficial, spontaneous, often large-scale activities and initiatives are becoming an important fact of national life.

Cultural life was the first arena for such spontaneous actions. Popular singers, officially frowned upon, found places to perform and the public located those venues without any announcements having been made. The best-known of these singers were Bulat Okudzava and the late Vladimir Vysotskii, but there are many others. And while the unofficial pop and rock bands are well known to readers of the Western press, there is also a host of unofficial theatrical groups.* Financed by neither the city nor the party, but sometimes by the local Komsomol league, these troupes often perform to capacity crowds, despite the lack of any publicity. In his latest

---

*Some of the rock bands have recently made quasi-official appearances, including on state television! The trend is clearly toward greater official recognition of many formerly unofficial social phenomena mentioned in this book.

book, Martin Walker paints a vivid picture of diverse unsanctioned events, including unofficial exhibitions of paintings in parks and metro stations [108:171]. Moreover, informal structures have proved able to overturn unwanted formal ones, as evidenced by the changes of guard, unopposed but not officially initiated, in the writers' union and the union of filmmakers.

All this, though, is only the tip of the iceberg, although the existence of avid and large publics ready for all kinds of lively unorthodox events, or orthodox but unofficial happenings, is relevant to the argument. But we may now turn to expressions of public opinion outside the cultural sphere. For example, there is now a large-scale, and initially quite spontaneous, public movement expressing disgust and horror at the ecological disasters and widespread pollution created as a byproduct of the relentless concentration on massive industrial projects. Ecology is now a catchword, and the ensuing debates and actions are a genuinely public affair.

Another example, less well known, is the increasing number of groups of scholars and other specialists in urban affairs who meet privately to work out solutions to the endless urban imbalances, insufficiencies, and social problems and to press their recommendations on the public and on the authorities. These days many think tanks are officially constituted government and academic bodies, but others initially emerge from the personal initiatives of colleagues or neighbors, or even on a broader interprofessional scale. New professional and interprofessional associations are appearing, and older official organizations are acquiring a new identity, shedding to some extent, at least, their official tutelage and expressing their own opinions.

More research is needed to detail these emerging phenomena. But it is already clear that urban reality is breeding a variety of groups, cultural trends, and institutions that are increasingly able to voice their opinions and press for their demands. The societal maze finds new ways to "keep private" what it wishes to have remain private, and to "socialize" what it does not want to have fully subject to statism.

We may sum up many of these phenomena as manifestations of an emerging civil society in the bosom of a system that is statist par excellence. By "civil society," we refer to the aggregate of networks and institutions that either exist and act independently of the state or are official organizations capable of developing their own, spontaneous views on national or local issues and then impressing these views on their members, on small groups and, finally, on the authorities. These social complexes do not necessarily oppose the state, but exist in contrast to outright state organisms and enjoy a certain degree of autonomy. The possibility of serious dissidence from various levels of society cannot be excluded.

Independent, informal trends and groups can and do also appear among the Soviet state bureaucracies. Public opinion, public moods and reactions penetrate state bodies and the party and meet with either opposition or sympathy from state officials. Though administrators have their own ebb and flow of opinions, they often do partake of the opinions prevalent in different strata of society at large.

The concept of a civil society operating in the very fortress of statism—among broad layers of officials, political opinion makers, and the party apparatus—challenges conventional thinking about the Soviet state. It is a novel idea about a novel situation. But insofar as administrators do belong to urban social groups, they may move in and out of the official and social worlds.

There is no doubt that many cultural and ideological trends, fashions, and political opinions now popular in Soviet society are shared by many in the apparatus. After all, the role models for youth, the publicly acknowledged status figures, are rarely apparatus people or political leaders. Rather, they are writers, scholars, specialists of impressive achievement, sports personalities, cosmonauts. The force of public opinion certainly impresses and sometimes even sways groups inside the apparatus. For although the apparaty insiders are often conservative and opposed to reforms and enlightened social change, they are not an island. Furthermore, civil society is not all light and progress; it can, and often does, support aggressive, oppressive, or dogmatic state action. Thus even the most conservative political leaders may be buoyed by substantial public support.

The topic of the Soviet Union's civil society merits serious attention. The analysis, however, must not be predicated on definitions, even though Hegelian propositions are not entirely irrelevant. But even at this point it is obvious that one-dimensional ideas about the Soviet system and its past, present, and future must be discarded. If the state is not the sole controller that it was thought to be, or hoped to be; if spontaneous historical trends and spontaneous public actions and reactions play a role in the making of the system; and if the USSR has developed a complex social body and a social system, with classes and publics, cultures and countercultures—then the political subsystem of such a complex aggregate must be understood to have a history of relating and responding to social and economic development. Moreover, the political subsystem has to be seen, especially in our times, as somewhat pliant, capable of changing its role in relation to the overall environment. It can and does press and make demands, but the institutions of the state do not unilaterally dictate the national agenda. More than ever before, the political organs are responding to the powerful contradictory pressures of domestic social reality as well as to the stresses and demands of international events.

Part Two

The New Course

7

The Social Sciences:
A New Ideology

In earlier chapters, we have gained many insights into social and urban problems from the works of Soviet social scientists. The evolution of Soviet social sciences in the last two decades is in itself a manifestation of the deep structural change that we have been examining. Social scientists, particularly under Gorbachev's aegis, have become a force on the Soviet social and cultural scene, informing and shaping public opinion as well as being part and parcel of the civil society. Though, as elsewhere, the social sciences are not accorded the same prestige as the natural sciences, and though Soviet scholarship is not yet on a par with the best Western work, the Soviet branches of sociology and social psychology, the much older branches of ethnography and demography (the latter having suffered great losses under Stalin), and such newcomers as systems analysis and political science are all on the move.

Not unlike the late fifties, when debates on proposed economic reforms contributed to the renaissance of So-

viet economics, notably of its mathematical branch
[61:137], social developments have spurred new forms of
scholarship. For example, urbanization and the accompanying transformation of social structures helped promote, revive, or create various branches of the social sciences in the USSR. Though studies of the countryside
continued, notably with more scholarly sophistication,
in the sixties the principal efforts were turned to the
study of the bewildering urban maze. In the seventies
and eighties impressive groups of scholars began to
break loose from the prevailing dogmas and half-truths
and initiated the serious study of sociology and other
disciplines.

Of course, sociologists were not particularly popular
with the authorities because of their tendencies to "seek
out problems." There are no more than 15,000 to 20,000
sociologists in the entire USSR, and the discipline is still
poorly taught in universities. The raw materials essential to their endeavors—social statistics—are scarce.
What statistical data there are, exist in the vaults of
the Statistical Agency—and this, says one author who
looks for such data, "does not count as social statistics"
[110].

Until recently, sociologists have also been handicapped by numerous taboos and restrictions on the
kinds of topics deemed fit for investigation and publication. A long list of such taboos, which Western scholars
have deplored for years, was presented in an article in
Pravda in February 1987 [110] by the indomitable Tatiana Zaslavskaia, a sociologist and member of the Academy of Sciences known for her outspokenness. In this article she reiterates her long-standing conviction—now
at long last also the official party line—that without
open debates of the most painful social problems, with-

out serious theoretical reflection and explanation, nothing can be solved. If sociology is to accomplish its mission—to unearth the root causes of complex social problems—sociologists must not be at every turn blocked by signs reading "Entry to Strangers Forbidden," as Zaslavskaia puts it.

Though Zaslavskaia paints the state of her discipline as still extremely weak, she is among the group of courageous and increasingly influential researchers who have laid the foundations for a new era in Soviet scholarship. Sociology has begotten a variety of subfields, the sociology of knowledge, of law, of culture, of art, parallel to those practiced in the West. And the city, heretofore of interest primarily to geographers, has attracted the attention of a whole bundle of Soviet scholarly disciplines including the very promising ethnosociology.

It goes without saying that these new fields borrowed massively from the West, English terms included, though older Russian Soviet works from the twenties were also relied upon. This was the price to be paid for the neglect or destruction of fields that had existed in the pre-Stalin period. That the borrowing is not always frankly acknowledged is not surprising, but Soviet researchers are already defining new problems, proposing original ideas, and making independent findings.

A propensity for mathematical models, from the start, has aided the newcomers in gaining respect in scientific circles. The creation of a more solid institutional setting—departments, academic institutes, somewhat improved schooling, and an influx of enthusiastic youth—has also promoted the quantity and quality of research in the social sciences. Perhaps the most influential expression of this enterprise, and an important mouthpiece of the reform-oriented intelligentsia, is the monthly *Sotsiologicheskie Issledovaniia* (Sociological Inquiries). Addressed to a readership beyond the professional public, this review publishes research findings as well as book reviews, bulletins, and short think pieces by sociologists, philosophers, historians, city planners, officials, and practitioners of different arts. From its inception in the 1970s, it has been an ever richer source of published and otherwise unpublished findings, of fresh data on a host of problems, and of conceptual work on social life, theories, structures, and systems. From the pages of this review one becomes aware of a growing stream of studies, from central and republican academies and universities, and hundreds of books on a vast array of topics: the main classes and functions of society, its micro and macro levels, from the family to youth and youth gangs, from management to workers and engineers, from bureaucracies to scientific institutes. Such topics now have their own literature and sociological surveys. The social, psychological, demographic, cultural, ecological, and psychopathological effects of industrialization, urbanization, migration, and crime are explored. Conferences, colloquia, and seminars are frequent; discussions and polemics on phenomena and concepts appear in print.

As an illustration, let us mention an intercity conference on the sociopsychological effects of scientific-technical progress on a range of human activities and relations. It was convened by the Central Research Sector on Social Psychology, one of the branches of the Soviet Sociological Association of the Academy of Sciences of the USSR, and the proceedings, representing the theoretical and empirical studies of sixteen scholars, were published in 1982 [78]. Among the array of topics discussed were: problems of labor and the collective, personality and collectivity, the adaptivity of individuals, the education of youth, mass communications and interpersonal relations, the social psychology of the family, psychological and social problems of leadership, demographic phenomena, and ethnicity.

The quality of this and other publications is often uneven, and a dogmatic cloud still hangs over some texts, at least in patches. But the production of the leading academic institutes is respectable, and for the first time scholarship is playing a decisive role in Soviet society. Barring some harsh political reversals, Soviet scholars of social thought are well on the road to becoming, in the near future, partners with their foreign colleagues.

Other fields are but in their teens. Political science (*politologiia*) had a particularly hard time establishing itself as an authorized discipline. The stranglehold of the branch called "state and law" (a term borrowed from Germany, before the revolution) was but one retarding factor. Today, however, the Academy of Sciences has its Association of Political Sciences and, like other fields, a yearbook. The new field may be forgiven for treading cautiously: when it comes to discussing the state, all fields of scholarship are still circumspect—none more so than "politologiia."

One can read, with bemusement, a political scientist's scolding of Max Weber for having proclaimed the inevitability of the bureaucratization of socialism. Weber is quoted as having said: "Up till now we could observe the triumphant march not of the dictatorship of the proletariat, but the dictatorship of the bureaucrat" [20:226]. We can only assume that this author disagrees with Weber. But he does, however, correctly present many of Weber's ideas, and his polemic against Weber is ambiguous.

Other political scientists have developed a more

roundabout way of flexing their muscle. Although many articles in the yearbooks respectfully examine Western theories, others propose extensive critiques of the Western Leviathan state and related political problems. Such studies allow their authors to master a considerable literature, to criticize freely a set of complicated, often negative, phenomena, and—when the time comes—to apply it all at home. In recent years a number of such critics of the West have substantially improved the quality of their work—no doubt a good training ground, and a double-edged sword.

Many branches of scholarship indulge far less in such feints and stratagems. To take a characteristic example, systems analysis, a rather new field but already well established and led by a strong institute in the Academy of Sciences, has been beneficial to all the social sciences. This field has not only propagated the value of systemic approaches but also supplied useful theoretical tools to its sister disciplines. Further, systems analysis by nature uses a language largely untainted by conventional ideological jargon. And researchers and theoreticians in this field have been able to confront problems that others are still shying away from. For example, when presenting the different laws of systems, a systems analyst can openly and directly, without much meandering, explain that laws do exist in social systems but that, as in the natural sciences, these laws are conceptualized as being irregular—a notion quite foreign to the withering official dogma.

This rebuff of the mechanistic conceptions of the previous era is just one example of how systems analysis helps dilute or even wash away the thick dogmatic sediments that once made serious thinking impossible.

More importantly, the new approach is helping to promote an altogether different ontological conception:
from the work of systems analysts a much more complex
world emerges, a world that demands a more strenuous
intellectual effort [39:317].

Stable patterns or laws do, of course, exist—otherwise
there would be no system. But an example will show
how the new language of systems analysis can raise, in
a way that politologiia as yet cannot, important political
problems inherent in the country's past and present policies. In a recent piece, analyst A. V. Katsura first in-
forms the reader of a law known in systems analysis as
the hypothesis of induced reaction [39:318]. Analogous
to Newton's third law of motion, this hypothesis asserts
that if a change (a disturbance) is introduced into a system, from outside or inside, that unsettles its stability, a
counteraction is triggered by the powerful mechanisms
of conservation. Numerous examples, Katsura continues, illustrate this point. Specifically, all revolutions
have provoked considerable counteraction from conservative forces, and some efforts to impose change by force
have provoked reactions more violent and damaging
than the initial disturbances.

Is this author a conservative, an opponent of revolution, or only opposed to revolutions against the Soviet
system? Or does he regret October? Be that as it may, he
is talking politics here: this law, according to him, ren-
ders futile—even pernicious—all kinds of voluntaristic
"leaps forward" or "economic miracles." The more
abrupt or powerful an action, the greater the potential
for a counteraction that could push the entire system
into a retrogressive phase. Right or wrong, this is not
just about Mao—it is about Stalin. And it serves as a cau-

tion to current policy makers: In introducing new policies, plan carefully and, above all else, don't rush, don't coerce!

For another example of the kind of work being undertaken, let us turn to the arguments of a sociologist, V. N. Ivanov, the director of the Research Institute in Social Interdisciplinary Studies of the Academy of Sciences. The institute is by now quite prestigious; its aim, as Ivanov shows [37:11–13], is to provide appropriate sociological backing for the official objective of "intensifying the economy." In this article Ivanov begins by drawing a troubling picture of an important social group: the engineers, an army of five million people. Beset by insufficiencies and inconsistencies of policy and structure (that is our way of putting it), notably poor labor organization and faulty methods of remuneration, engineers are unable to perform their work efficiently. The prestige of the profession is dwindling, engineers are quitting and taking jobs in which their skills are underutilized or forfeited. According to studies, the phenomenon affects 40 percent of university graduates in engineering and 75 percent of the graduates of technical colleges. Moreover, the quality of instruction and preparation of young specialists has recently fallen off.

How to cope with such a situation, what to do, where are the bottlenecks? Sociology is asked to contribute. Surveys have shown that had circumstances allowed, many respondents could have and would have improved their work performance, though a considerable number of workers were apathetic. Ivanov cites one such survey of over two thousand workers in fourteen enterprises located in four regions of the country.

In order to examine problems of such national magnitude, sociologists must clarify many practical, empirical, and theoretical points. Broadly, the focus must be the essence of the "social sphere" and its interrelation with the economy, complemented by an understanding of people's interests and needs. The social factors requisite to accelerating economic performance have to be explored and methods proposed to activate them. Unfortunately, all these crucial social factors, the author reminds us, have been neglected. They were the weak link in the social sciences and in state policies; now, that link must be quickly fortified.

Similar themes are, of course, also subjects of larger national debate. But Ivanov mentions one rather new development that promises to lend more practical substance to the sociological profession. Some five thousand sociologists are already at work in "services of social development" that thirty ministries have adopted and instituted at all levels of their hierarchy (central, intermediary, and local).

Another voice in the national debate is added by social psychology. Sociopsychological researchers, combining, as others do, micro- and macrodimensions, are deeply worried by the depersonalizing forces of modern urban life. Studies of the workplace—of factory shop floors, offices, and scientific institutes—stress the need to strengthen the world of the individual and the lives of small collectives as an antidote to labor productivity problems caused by poor morale ("sociopsychological climate"). Morale in the workplace, the researchers note, affects far more than productivity, since the workplace is the prime shaper of an individual's self-image and identity.

Labor incentives and motivations come under scrutiny in numerous studies, as does management style. Here one finds almost unanimous opposition to authoritarian styles of management, which are still quite wide-spread in the Soviet Union. Such methods, the social scientists often report, breed demoralization and lower productivity, induce anxiety and neurosis among the workforce, and produce widespread symptoms of dissatisfaction with the workplace or the work itself. In the eyes of managers and politicians, such bold antiauthoritarian attitudes may be dismissed as sowing the seeds of laxity and sloppiness, effecting the breakdown of discipline, and pampering the labor force into laziness. But the logic of much scholarly thinking seems set: modern tasks demand a highly skilled, well-educated population, and management methods must adapt to this new reality. (Presumably, this rule holds for all enterprises, except perhaps the army.) Public opinion is also now a factor in the workplace. The boss may be nominated from above, but if he does not have public approval from below, it is argued, he will fail [78:140–43].

We would expect a similar conclusion to follow in regard to higher levels of management and the political system at large. This inescapable line of thought is already at least implied in the texts. The practical problems that such studies are raising, concerning past and current sources of weakness and the generally low level of effectiveness in the system, lead, in sum, to a more detailed picture of how the system actually functions and what appear to be the main trouble spots. Whatever the level of inquiry, this kind of work demands and yields the theoretical concepts without which a deeper understanding of the whole "mechanism" cannot be attained nor serious in-depth proposals for change be formulated. We have already seen how systems analysis—a branch that is, by definition, highly theoretical—offers pioneering ideas for broader generalizations. The systemic approach, heartily welcomed by Soviet social scientists and acceptable to any serious Marxist, has a direct bearing on the political domain and poses implications for the shape of the political system.

Though scholarship in the social sciences suffers from disciplinary fragmentation and is capable of producing visions no less one-sided than those of the oft-criticized administration, scholars believe that they are capable of interdisciplinary collaboration and that they alone will be able to provide policy makers with the necessary research and theory on sociocultural complexities. The scholars' basic message to policy makers is clear: Administrations can administer only so much and can grasp from their own experience only some of the current problems of their routine. The analysis of complicated social processes is beyond their ability—but such processes and long-term social trends, including psychological and cultural tendencies, are the main forces that shape people and situations, create the problems, and define the nation's historical and current agenda.

Ideas like that and terms like *complexity* and *spontaneity*, which scholars are also trying to make the politicians acknowledge, hit hard at the weakest spots of Soviet political experience and practice. Historically, the state system has been geared toward regulation and controls, but social development can be regulated by administrations only up to a point, and many human affairs, large and small, are not amenable to state planning. These matters should be understood by policy makers, but then either left to social initiative or supported (or counteracted) by an adequate infrastructure and left to their own devices, unless some phenomena take on menacing proportions.

Ethnicity is one example of social expression not

amenable to state control. As one social scientist argues, ethnic solidarities and identities of national minorities in Soviet cities "are the result of primarily natural, spontaneous historical processes" [92:44] and need no administrative regulation. Even if these processes, or the preference of authorities, point to assimilation in the future, it is not appropriate to meddle in the deeper sociopsychological structures that underlie an ethnic group's collective identity. If the state is to take any action, it should be to create the necessary conditions supportive of the specificity of individual ethnic groups [92:44].

This author was speaking specifically about Tatar minorities in Leningrad and Moscow. But the implications go beyond just the ethnic problems in the USSR and aim, more broadly, at the relations between the state and its societal partners and hurdles. In a wide variety of complicated, often subtle relations, political leaders must learn to grapple with difficult concepts, say, "the psychosocial infrastructure"—which means history, tradition, culture, and habits of the population [92:40].

The need to understand an immense social field beyond economic and political controls and to apply this knowledge to the formation and application of policy constitutes a novel and difficult challenge to politicians and administrators. "Personality," its needs and freedoms, the rights and interests of small collectives of different types, and respect for public opinion—the curriculum is quite demanding. And if one adds the postulates of freedom of movement and communications and free access to information, the request for change in the polity seems so thoroughgoing that one wonders whether these scholars have any real hope. Yet again, these expectations are supplemented (the economists are here also quite helpful) by demands for integrated administration and planning—that is, planning that will integrate the vertical and horizontal links, the local and national, the economic and social—to remedy the interminable incoherences the Soviet system suffers from.

In all these scholarly admonitions about current Soviet policies, the "human factor" is one of the key points of departure. One social scientist invokes this concept in an effort to return the Soviet system to its initial ideological promise, a proposition characteristic of earlier endeavors to reform the system. In Soviet conditions, this author counsels, the social nature of a working person has two tightly interconnected aspects: he is "a worker and, simultaneously, a co-owner of the means of production." It turns out, though, that in real life these two aspects are not as tightly knit as the formula would have it. Sufficient attention has not yet been paid, either in practice or in theory, to the second aspect, the author explains, adding that the effectiveness of any economic reorganization will depend on the way this problem is approached [37:15].

Such are some of the ideas that various Soviet social scientists are proposing in order to arrest the decline of the system and help revitalize it. We should emphasize that many of the formulations cited here antedate Gorbachev's era by ten to twenty years. But only since 1985 have the renascent social sciences truly begun to flourish. Earlier political leaders did not want their scholars bothering about the intricacies of small-scale and large-scale social life. Some academics did their work anyway, and today their participation is officially encouraged—certainly a moment of great satisfaction for the brighter and more forward-looking scholars. And from their work is emerging far more than just data and hypotheses about society. Every empirical study of existing conditions—whether about the family or neighborhood groups, conditions of scientific creativity or conditions for productivity in industry, or the quality of services and the psychology of the relations between salespersons and buyers in state stores—is followed by ever more explicit demands for broad change, improvement, and further reflection and hypothesizing.

The concept of human capital—used in the West for some time already—acquires in the Soviet polity an importance beyond the nature of human relations between labor and management in the workplace. What is involved here is a profound change in existing relations of authority and hierarchy in the system. It is a revision—and a reminder that the ruling party has strayed from some basic principles.

In addition, the human capital thesis—the idea that people, the basic capital of the nation, have to be treated appropriately—is enriched by the other themes we have been discussing: respect for the spiritual side of the individual, easy access to necessary information, enhanced mobility and choice of professional opportunities, and a role for public opinion in policy making. Taken as one bundle, these programmatic requests imply that the human capital thesis relates not just to people as economic producers, but even more so, as citizens.

One formulation of such a program propounds the urgent task of improving "the entire social environment." As the arguments evolve and new empirical studies are conducted to buttress the reformers' theses, a sociopolitical philosophy, an ideology, is coalescing in intellectual, notably scholarly, circles. And the new program is finding support among the political leadership. Is this a renewal of a Soviet version of humanism, is it a "liberalism" Soviet style? That remains to be seen. After all, the new approaches are now officially sanctioned. We cannot yet distinguish between those who are acting from sincerely felt convictions and those who are simply acquiescing to the new official line, self-defensively conforming to the latest fashion in official attitudes.

The coming years will test the truth, and especially the practicality, of the new scholarship. Will their methodology enable Soviet social scientists to offer good advice? Will their advice be accepted? Will it be sufficient to effect substantive change? Here we may return to Zaslavskaia, whom some see as a driving force behind many of the changes now envisaged or in progress. A revolutionary restructuring (*perestroika*) is already under way, she contends; that it is revolutionary is attested to by the fact "that a battle of enormous intensity 'for' and 'against' the perestroika is being joined" [110]. Sociology's role, she explains, is to supply the analysis of and remedies for social, economic, and other problems, to anticipate difficulties and provide alternatives. She even appeals for "a constant sociological supervision over the execution of decisions taken and over the way in which the concrete processes of the reforms are proceeding."

But there is another task that Zaslavskaia urges sociology to attend to. The Soviet people are mired in the widespread apathy inherited from previous governments. Sociology can be of help in the "activization of the human factor" by inspiring habits of social thinking in the population. In a vision almost Promethean, she reminds her readers of the enormous resources that were devoted to harnessing the atom for peaceful uses, and yet, "releasing the social energy of the human masses, steering it into socially useful channels is a task, certainly not lesser in scale, and probably not of lesser complexity. And this task falls upon the shoulders of sociologists before anybody else."

Are sociology and other social sciences destined to become in the Soviet Union what John Kenneth Galbraith thought the scientific community would become in the West—"a fourth estate"? In the Soviet case it would probably be only a second or third estate; in the West it has not happened yet. But these are good, creative, ambitious dreams for a country just awakening from a long slumber.

Let us note, in closing, an interesting paradox. When the USSR was at its most coercive and "voluntaristic," it professed, in theory, a rigid, mechanistic determinism. Now, when it wants to move from an "extensive" to an "intensive" stage, it seems ready to replace a dogmatic determinism with a philosophically more flexible notion of causality, to replace the principles of certainty with those of probability and accept more accident-prone "laws" of history. The effect of such changes of perspective on longer-term politics remains to be seen. In intellectual life, the new ideology is already gathering momentum.

8

"Planned Imbalances," the Making of a Crisis

After Stalin died, the political system, heavily corrupted and incapacitated by his rule, was badly in need of repair. The economy was a shambles: the standard of living of the masses was lamentable, and agricultural production was at or below the per capita standards of tsarist Russia. The party was in disarray, and the top leaders maneuvered nervously lest they be destroyed in the battle for power by more adept players—Beria was clearly the most menacing of all.

Under Khrushchev's leadership, however erratic his later performance, considerable normalization of the political process occurred and a slow start was made to improve the lot of the population. His first task as head of the presumably ruling party, such as it was, was to reestablish the party's power. For under Stalin the party had lost power to the dictator and to anyone he fancied to promote. Party institutions—the Central Committee, congresses, even the Politbureau—worked only as told and when told. Even when these institutions met, party officials merely rubber-stamped what had been done in their name. Not much of a ruling party, by all accounts.

Thus it was left to Khrushchev to restore the institutions of the party. Over several years, government bodies recovered their authority and self-assurance, and a host of reforms were initiated. The earliest changes concerned mostly the functioning of the top bureaucracy, the main social force backing the normalization. To reaffirm and guarantee their right and ability to exercise power, this echelon introduced a certain "constitutionalism" in the functioning of party and state administrations. No more one-man rule; no cumulation of the positions of general secretary and prime minister; an end to the purges, the wanton killings and imprisonment of alleged "enemies of the people"; an end to the rule of terror from top to bottom. Rather, collective leadership, predictable tenures in office, and enhanced attention to the rule of law.

This regularization of the functioning of bureaucracy proved beneficial to the entire population. The concentration camps were emptied of millions of innocent or not-too-guilty inmates. The power of the secret police was curtailed drastically. Codes were prepared and enacted, and the slowly recovering juridical profession soon resembled a lobby, featuring some bold spokesmen who pressed for more rights for the profession and for its clients. Long lists of changes and improvements followed, and the upswing lasted some fifteen years.

The key political changes in the USSR during this period did not escape Western observers. As one specialist on Soviet politics concluded in 1979, most political scientists in the U.S. agreed "at least on one basic point, namely, that actual power is now not as concentrated in the top political leadership as it once was and has diffused downwards to some extent" [30:548]. Nonetheless, one of the prevailing approaches in Western sovietology (represented by Zbigniew Brzezinski and Samuel P. Huntington) saw basically just "oligarchical petrification." The challenging school ventured, for the first time, into some concept of a Soviet political process based on "interest groups" among the bureaucrats (H. Gordon Skilling and Franklyn Griffiths), although such behavior had been standard procedure even under the darkest days of Stalinism. Jerry Hough's perceptive discussion of institutional pluralism was largely ignored, appearing too farfetched to the bulk of kremlinologists who dominated the public debate. (Hough persisted, though, and his concept allowed him to discern in the Soviet system even some kind of "constitutional restraints" [30:554–55].)

Of course, Western analysts were handicapped by the lack of information available. But, in any case, observations that confined themselves to the top of the hierarchy could not yield insights into the regime's trajectory. For the most dynamic events were taking place outside the Kremlin, in the social sphere, well beyond the view of most political scientists.

In the USSR, in the meantime, the upper bureaucratic layers, though now larger and better trained, began losing their dynamism. The bureaucrats who had normalized the system—and, to a large extent, the entirety of national life—settled into complacency, enjoying their power and positions. Having obtained all they wanted, they quickly fell into routine and often corrupt ways. The virtuous effort in the 1960s to reform the economy—either the swan song of the bureaucracy's good intentions or, maybe, the first effort of their reformist wing—

was scuttled. All the nation's vital functions—economic performance, political leadership, ideological vitality—were declining dangerously and refusing any standard remedies. Throughout the social and political spectrum, symptoms of a damaging "motivational crisis" appeared, demoralizing the population and the cadres—a theme we will pick up after discussing some of the causes of the malaise.

At the heart of the malfunctions in the economy, in politics, and in other areas was the long-standing phenomenon—often deplored in the press and in books—of *vedomstvennost'*. *Vedomstvo* (plural, *vedomstva*) means "department," and the disease is therefore one of "departmentalism," an ailment that plagued the entire so-called mechanism of managing crucial national business. It connotes, first of all, the ministries, especially the economic ones, but also other power organizations, including important enterprises.

In the 1930s the ministries emerged as leaders of the main branches of the economy, including the construction industries that built the cities. Even today the ministerial bureaucracy is the main national entrepreneur, responsible for the well-being of the labor force and the disposition of most of the nation's investment and working capital.

All along, the ministries' planning and management systems were based on the principle of verticalism: hierarchical pyramids, centralized in Moscow, direct enterprises and administrations throughout the USSR. Each subordinate jurisdiction communicates only with the office above it in the same ministry; no meaningful direct communication takes place between neighboring enterprises and institutions that belong to different ministries. This absence of horizontal links is a source of great trouble to this day, because so much of the functioning of a healthy system is, of course, horizontal by definition. When the most powerful presence in a city are enterprises subordinated to one or more vedomstva and there is no horizontal coordination, staggering inconsistencies, incoherences, and imbalances result. The same maladaptive schema governs the entire national economy and many other areas of national life.

Although common knowledge since the very day the Soviet departments emerged, officials have finally timidly acknowledged that each vedomstvo so develops its own interests and techniques for quashing competing claims that ultimately the national interest may count for nothing. In Moscow there is, sometimes, power enough to impose a national perspective on local or regional disputes. But from day to day the vedomstva are supposed to be representatives of the national interest. A theorist gives several examples [20:62–63]. Suppose a local government wants to keep an area of fertile land for agricultural use, but the vedomstvo prefers to allocate the land for other purposes. The vedomstvo always wins out, for local and city governments are no match for the powerful central agencies. Similarly, in disputes over opening or closing plants, the ministry or big industrial firm always has its way, despite local needs or national interests. Even if there is an appropriate law on the books, the local authorities cannot enforce it against the central agency because the city or town stands to lose too much, in terms of housing, schools, and amenities, if it antagonizes the powerful central source of funds.

Another example. Factories located in one city often belong to different ministries, and their activities are therefore not coordinated. The result is that such cities are effectively split into "disconnected and poorly managed 'microcities,' " which journalists call "manufacturing villages," while "scholarly literature dubs them 'departmental blurs' " [9:52–53].

Some of the most vexing problems of urbanization and town building are being traced to the same vedomstvennost that has afflicted communal construction. A professor complained in *Pravda* ten years ago, and a sociologist found it worth quoting five years later, about the city of Bratsk in Siberia: "Bratsk is one of the most graphic and depressing demonstrations of departmental chaos: it consists of a dozen workers' settlements distant from each other and almost isolated from each other, belonging to different ministries. In addition to offering poor living conditions, constructing it cost much more than anticipated. Yet it is impossible to find who was responsible for all this" [15:190]. Bratsk, built between 1955 and 1973, today has 220,000 inhabitants and cascading imbalances: more industrial plant than labor, more labor than housing and schools, and far more men than women.

In response to such incoherence (*rassoglasovannost'*), Soviet citizens vote with their feet: they walk away. Labor turnover and internal migration tell the story. This is a good moment to remind ourselves that freedom to move inside the country and change jobs is a long-established and frequently used right of the Soviet citizen.

The troubles of cities are only one aspect of the system's propensity for disorganization, despite its claims to planning. No one is surprised to learn that the rogue-elephant vedomstva have long ignored "the delicate mechanisms of the environmental impact on social processes" [34:42]. But the implicit accusation, which others voice loudly these days, is that the ecological disasters that befall the country have to be put squarely at the doorsteps of the departments—and the departments *are* the government. Malfunctions and imbalances, disincentives and disproportions also shackle the economy, the conduct of science, and the professionalization of the labor force and the bureaucracy. A memoir written by an "outstanding worker" shows how the pay system discourages productivity and initiative, how the vaunted "socialist competition," an old story already, turns into an exercise of bureaucratic make-believe [5:165–67]. Inadequate planning leaves factories and scientific institutions with too few technicians to assist the highly qualified specialists, causing much stress to the specialists and often their de facto dequalification [90:254].

Thus far, numerous government efforts to correct such imbalances have had little or no effect. By now both scholars and government experts agree that the whole economic system is unproductively hoarding masses of labor and materials; factories often keep working "for the warehouse," accumulating piles of unsalable goods, even as the nation is beset by shortages [2:4]. Worse, the economy operates under a prevailing pull to produce *zatraty*; that is, enterprises focus on costs and expenditures rather than income and profits. In other words, the economy favors waste and is therefore, by definition, uneconomical. Hence the search to change the mechanism into an "anti-*zatratnyi* one" [18:31].

As we move from observing the symptoms to writing out the diagnosis, let us first turn to one of the most interesting recent theoretical contributions by the well-known Hungarian economist Jànos Kornai. In a still only partly worked-out model of Soviet-style economies, Kornai describes the system as primarily investment oriented, a propensity that necessarily produces permanent shortages [51]. This does not mean, Kornai states, that such a system is basically unworkable. Despite its inefficiencies, it is capable of growth, can successfully address many needs of the citizenry, and even boasts some advantages over Western economies.

What Kornai's model, at least in its preliminary form, does not show is whether there are inherent limits to the functioning of the system. In the case of the USSR, we know that as the economy grew so did the malfunctions and disproportions until, finally, the malfunctions multiplied faster than the economy expanded. One sign of the progressing sclerosis is that in recent years the accumulation of unsold and unsalable goods clogging the warehouses grew two to three times faster than the output of industry [2:4].

Modern theories of economic management stress integrative planning that coordinates and correlates the vertical and horizontal links in a national economy. Some Soviet writers use the term *kompleksnyi*, that is, systemic approach [15:190]. But the present planning system is not capable of this, indeed is breeding the opposite, *nesbalansirovannost'* (imbalances).

The harsh verdict of Soviet academics and leaders today on the planning and managing of the economy also singles out the system's inability to handle "structural shifts" [2:4]. Now that the economy and society are complex, intricately enmeshed entities, they can no longer tolerate such ineffectiveness: "The predominantly branch-oriented framework of management and planning undermines the interests of harmonious development in the cities" [53:35–36].

The problem, though, is not just the system's inability to organize urban construction and development. The entire economic oversight mechanism is faulty and has to be replaced. The political leaders have come to this conclusion, too. But the problem does not stop with the economic system. For example, why can't the powerful central government tame the vedomstva? Why have repeated government efforts to reform the economy never succeeded in reversing the rising tide of imbalances and dysfunctions?

Part of the answer rests in the defensive strategies any system develops to ensure self-preservation; systems acquire a self-sustaining momentum. In the case of the planning system, the planners' initial concentration was on priorities in the economy, and they produced the best framework and method they could: the pyramids of ministerial and administrative agencies.

But in due course, as anticipated by Trotsky in *The New Course* (1923–1924), the party apparatus merged with the state bureaucracy. The key consequence of this merger was the transformation of the party apparatus. Organized so as to be able to control the government, the party apparatus succumbed to the pattern it was supervising. It became addicted to the "branch principle" itself. Instead of remaining the controller, it became not just "etatized," as Trotsky and later Bukharin observed, but also an adjunct of the economic bureaucracy. It thereby lost its political character and was transformed into a basically economistic administration.

This happened during the Stalin era, when a governing matrix emerged that tightly united the bureaucratic networks of the party-state-economy axis. This matrix acquired a considerable rigidity, notably because it accomplished important things and retained a monopoly on assessing and praising itself. Although considerably diluted in the post-Stalin period, the key matrix persevered and *vedomstvennost'* flourished—the party itself was hooked on it.

As we have seen, this dominant matrix neglected spontaneous social developments, important social structural requirements, and the maze of the microforms. At the same time, obsessed with controls, it blocked many autonomous social organizations, thereby depriving itself of the feedback and resources of the growing society.

Too much state and too little social autonomy was surely one of the causes of the widespread crisis of values: job dissatisfaction, disappointed and frustrated youth, cynicism and self-interest, psychic and criminal deviance, drinking and drug taking—a multitude of problems that the state was not capable of coping with and that often were none of its business anyway. One may also speak of a "motivational crisis," a term borrowed from Jürgen Habermas's "motivational pattern," which posits the incompatibility of moral systems derived from different stages of capitalist development [27:185ff.]. The rapidity of changes in all facets of Soviet life "condensed" social forces, cultural patterns, and moral attitudes from different stages of development in an uneasy coexistence.

The state, riveted to its preferred national macrodimensions, lost sight of the microworld. There, in the depth of the social system, the moral crisis festered and raged until it finally spilled over into the workplace at all levels and sectors. The acute problem of poor morale (sociopsychological climate) in the workplace was the irrefutable indicator of the state's loss of economic stamina, political vigor, and ideological credibility. Depleted reserves of accessible raw materials, a demoralized labor force, ever less goodwill in the population—the extensive methods had "overextended" themselves.

When Gorbachev and the new leadership announced a new call "to intensify," to improve quality, one conclusion was inescapable: the quality of the government had to change first. For this purpose, more than the economistic matrix had to give way. The accretion that had annexed itself to the basic matrix, namely the "party-state-ideology-culture" amalgam, had to go as well; it was dying anyway.

9

The Way Out: A New Line

As we have seen, Gorbachev inherited a system in trouble. Yet the government was stable and not menaced in any way either from inside or from outside. For a new leadership bent on undertaking a process of renovation, this situation was probably propitious. The dangers were on the horizon, visible to competent observers and politicians, but the state machinery was still in control and the citizenry, though often bitter, was not at all rebellious.

The crisis had been created by the mechanisms of economic management that had emerged in the 1930s and were still powerful. The new leaders saw the problem clearly: the party had been sponsoring the state machine, but in the process the political arm had become an adjunct of the economic machinery, rather than the other way around. The political agency had succumbed, become "economized" [62:32–34], and political leadership had been relegated to three deeply enmeshed bureaucracies, state-economy-party, that rigidly and mechanically applied the methods used in economic management to all problems it faced. This single-mindedness had succeeded for a time, but had by now turned into a trap. The national leadership had failed to develop ways of adapting to and dealing with the crucially important spheres of society and culture. As the newly urbanized society took shape, it began placing pressure on the governing model, insisting that each sphere of action receive the attention it needed and that new institutions and new methods be created to serve the new social forms. The system needed to "loosen up."

Because the basic triad, with its predominantly administrative approach, could not handle the emerging social, ideological, cultural, and even political tasks, the government began to suffer from the illness of "overloading." Overburdened and lacking the necessary resources to cope with ever new sets of tasks, the state-economy-party triad began to lose its efficiency in the economic sphere. In a parallel sphere, as noted above, the triad of power-ideology-culture was becoming bankrupt even faster than the economy. The primitive propaganda, the monolithic and simplistic ideology, the crude distortions of reality, and the heavy controls of culture and information—unmistakable signs of a politically underdeveloped system—began to produce worsening symptoms of a crisis of legitimacy.

That the government remained stable can be explained by, among other factors, the considerable achievements the system had made over time in many vital sectors. The USSR had become a superpower, had educated its population, and had created a machinery of state that ably managed important routine tasks and excelled at handling emergencies. Paradoxically, the Chernobyl catastrophe, which no doubt resulted from incompetence and sloppiness, also showed the world how effectively the Soviet government could respond to an unprecedented emergency. An official of the International Atomic Energy Agency concluded that "there were grave and flagrant errors that caused the accident, but once the accident occurred the problems were tackled with great intelligence and a tremendous amount of muscle" [76].

We do not know much about the personalities at the top and their thinking during the last years of Brezhnev's administration. Martin Walker has provided many new details [108] and suggests that much rethinking may have taken place in meetings between, among others, Yuri V. Andropov, then a Politbureau member and chief of the K.G.B., and a bright young party leader from the Stavropol area, Mikhail Gorbachev. Alliances adumbrated and ideas shared at that time might have prepared the way for the transitional period under Konstantin U. Chernenko, when Gorbachev was, in fact, already running the whole show. The new line that was announced by Gorbachev when he became general secretary startled the world, but it was by no means an overnight improvisation.

The new line, to begin with, was characterized by an appeal for frankness. The leaders were ready to look unflinchingly at the truth and to report to the country that the system was in bad shape. Their judgment of the economic mechanism was categorical: it was useless. Of course, the Party Congress put it more mildly, but still quite unambiguously: "The production relations that exist currently, the system of husbanding and managing, emerged, in substance, in conditions of extensive economic development. Gradually, they became obsolete, lost their stimulating power and turned, in many ways, into a hindrance" [2:5].

But the new line did not stop with criticisms of the management of the economy. Ideology and ideological life were also described as being in shambles. The Soviet people, the leaders admitted, did not believe official statements, and ideological dogma, though lifeless, was a powerful impediment to the country's development. Public initiative had been stifled, the public felt excluded from decisions, and the public had been lied to all too often. The system was ideologically vulnerable and unacceptably backward.

That much criticism, stated openly or implied, was more than the Soviet people had ever heard from their leaders. But soon much that had at first been implied was stated openly and sharply. Teachers of social sciences and ideological disciplines were summoned and reprimanded for having perpetuated the dogmatic and irrelevant clichés that were at the root of the system's current troubles. A Politbureau member told the assembled instructors that a survey conducted among university students found (as everyone already knew) that the ideological courses were boring and were conducted without any discussion. Students were not at all convinced by dogmatic formulas on "scientific communism" and similar disciplines.

The lecturers were also accused of "lacking civic courage" because it was their task to expose the country's burning problems, not to camouflage them. Gorbachev himself spoke on this same theme, maybe even to the same assembly: the teaching of many socio-ideological disciplines had become "something boring, formal, bureaucratic"—he used the untranslatable term *kazënnoe*

—whereas the order of the day was now "the breaking of former stereotypes" [64.4–5].

This was, in itself, an admission of a crisis, and the party was at the center of it. The new leaders were ready to state this, too: the party was no more than an economic apparatus, a carbon copy of the ministerial bureaucracies, which had long ceased fulfilling their proper political responsibilities. And the list of criticisms, admissions, and disclosures only continued to grow. In the wake of Gorbachev's appeal for serious and critical public debate on national problems—the well-known slogan for it is *glasnost'*—the press began to report on new disclosures and problems.

As the critique expanded and deepened, the leadership took its first moves in the new direction. In a step of considerable boldness, the government attacked the appalling problem of alcohol abuse. This was followed—how else?—by a public debate. Although many predicted failure, the government stuck to its guns, gained public support for its aims and, thus far, the anti-drinking campaign, despite setbacks, has achieved some success. This was a clever and promising opening.

Together with the appeal for glasnost—a slogan but also a pledge to ease censorship and facilitate access to information—there was a call for *uskorenie*, a speeding up of the pace of economic development, especially technological progress. Specific programs and blueprints for reforms have been proposed by numerous high-level committees and councils, and some of these plans are already under way: reforms concerning higher education, the economy, research and development, cultural life, national ministries and services (the national statistical service, for instance). Reviews are being made of legislation and penal policies, of a range of social policies, and of the party apparatus—probably soon of party life in general. The activity, without being precipitous, is feverish. Nonetheless, some Western observers still claim that "nothing really happens," that there is no well-defined program, notably for economic reforms. But that is sheer obstinacy. Ideas for change are being debated, implemented, and tested. That no comprehensive program has been announced seems rather a good sign. For what single program could fill the bill?

The Soviet leadership has already begun to act on its pledge to better inform the public. This openness is a precondition for the success of a further postulate, by now almost a new political credo: serious attention to public opinion is seen as the first step toward both democratization and the improving of "the political and moral climate in society at large" [64:12]. The Central Committee, says a party secretary, Politbureau member Egor Ligachev, "has reached conclusions of strategic importance concerning the growing role of the social sphere, the broadening of democracy . . . ways of developing the socialist self-rule of the people and activizing political and ideological institutions" [64:16].*

The very new and ultimately decisive "strategic orientation toward the social sphere" is presented in official documents as "the key to the accelerated solution of numerous problems, current and future, of our life" [84:3]. The social reforms under consideration range from improvements in living conditions and social services to the creation and implementation of a broad demographic policy, to a new philosophy of respect for personal dignity and human rights.

All the organizations and institutions are being reminded of their true missions and are being called upon to fulfill them. Trade unions, soviets, workers' assemblies, and groups in factories—everywhere the searching light of glasnost, of debate and criticism, encourages reform and improvements under close public scrutiny.

To make it all credible, the party itself is criticized for neglecting one of its main duties, social justice. The theory and the practice of social justice is explored in learned journals, and the press reports breaches with vigor. The privileges, hidden benefits, and supply networks that the leading cadres permitted themselves are now openly attacked. Such perquisites, says a philosopher, "violate socialist principles of distribution and therefore produce social discontent and tension" [84:8]. The system of indulgences deeply offended people's sense of justice and discredited the upper layers in government and the party.

The new Moscow party secretary and Politbureau candidate Boris Yeltsin has spoken to the Party Congress about problems of social justice with a sense of embarrassment and sadness. Those problems, he stated, are discussed by working people passionately and sharply: "One feels ill at ease when listening to expressions of indignation against any form of injustice—current ones or those already quite encrusted. But it is particularly painful when people speak directly of the special advantages for leaders" [84:9]. When party leaders lose their sense of duty and modesty, they lapse into what the new line calls *razlozhenie*, "degeneration," a sharp invective against people in power who use their positions for their own purposes and betray their social and political responsibility.* (*Razlozhenie*, we may note, was used in the 1920s by critics of the party protesting similar abuses of power. Those critics, as we know, met a sad fate.)

---

*Boris Yeltsin entered into a conflict with Gorbachev and is now a leader of the oppositional group of deputies in the new People's Congress. He still retains his seat in the Central Committee of the Communist Party. [M.L., January 1990]

Those much-resented privileges that big bosses arrogated to themselves included supplies of foreign or other goods not available to the public, access to special hospitals and other services, better schools, cozy restaurants. Neither the intelligentsia nor the rank and file deny that responsible leaders and specialists deserve high salaries. But, all agree that salaries should be public knowledge and that hidden benefits should be prohibited. And such reforms are now under way.

Why did the party tolerate such widespread corruption? Why was the party unable to control the self-indulgent bosses? Did the party actively persecute people who tried to expose the abuses? We know that many in the leadership abhorred the abuses and did not participate in them. But there was a group of apologists who "theorized" that the system of privileges was unavoidable as long as shortages existed. The Yeltsins, some of the more puritanical breed now in power, reject such maneuvers firmly. Time will show whether "clean" power is possible. But it is still up to the party as a whole to explain why it tolerated and even allowed large-scale corruption to flourish.

We must also mention the new thaw in the arts and culture. *Thaw* is the term conventionally used, but even on this score we are hearing something new. Ligachev took up this theme at the Twenty-seventh Party Congress in relation, not just to culture, but to freedom of criticism in general: "In the past, comrades," he stated, "as is well known, in this kind of thing, *we had 'freezes' and 'thaws', but what we really need is, quite simply, steady good weather"* [18;237].

Glasnost, democratization, self-government in the workplace, orientation to the social sphere, social justice, human rights, and respect for human individuality: the scope and spirit of the emerging reforms is almost too broad to be believed. But it also is too insistent to be dismissed as rhetoric or window dressing. On the threshold of a new era in its history, the nation's elders and a growing portion of the population know that nothing less than a vast vision of comprehensive change will suffice. The new line, Gorbachev declared, is enjoying growing public support—a support, he claimed, "we haven't enjoyed for decades" [16:14].

Anatoly F. Dobrynin, former Soviet envoy to the United States, now secretary to the Central Committee, sums up the new line by quoting Gorbachev: "what we need is more dynamism, more social justice, more democracy—in a word, more socialism" [16:20].

That is quite bold. One does not try to mobilize people, institute new freedoms, engage in far-reaching reforms (deeply resented by many), sweep out the old guard, and make quite dangerous promises and appeals in order to score a point or gain popularity. This program is a battle cry; it is serious and risky. Risky, because no single formula or blueprint can guide the vast project of revitalizing the entire system. Almost every point has to be improvised, tested out, and openly debated. "Rethinking" everything—another new slogan—is the rallying call. The entire political structure needs mending or scrapping and replacing; the Soviet Union must come to terms with a new, not entirely understood—and for some, even menacing—society; a host of other problems, national and international, are also looming large.

But the opposition groups are mounting, and the ensuing battle cannot be conducted and will not be worthwhile for stakes less than an all-embracing program for transformation. Although "rethinking" is a refreshing slogan for a leader to launch anywhere these days (we haven't heard anything like it for quite some time in the modern political arena), we must ask ourselves whether all this is possible. The new line goes well beyond the ideas raised during the last burst of intellectual and political effervescence, in the 1960s. Then the focus was on economic reforms, the political implications of which were only stealthily becoming manifest.

Times have changed, and much time was probably also wasted. In the past twenty-five years the range and magnitude of problems have increased, and the scope of proposed changes must now match that. In fact, when reflecting on all that is involved, one cannot help thinking that Gorbachev's task looks so formidable as to be just short of impossible. In assessing his chances, in the following chapters, we must proceed with a certain degree of caution.

---

*Egor Ligachev, the number two on the Politbureau, supported fully the Gorbachev line in early 1987. Later he seemed to have dissented on the degree of *glasnost'* and democratization and was removed to a recently created Agricultural Department, away from ideology and supervision of the party apparatus. But he remains on the Politbureau and is still probably quite influential.

10

Gorbachev's Challenge

The political program announced by Gorbachev is clearly an effort to respond to the new realities of Soviet society. For although Soviet society has changed greatly in the last three decades, the ruling state system, which had been shaped in a different setting, continued in its old ways, its methods coming to look ever more antediluvian.

The backwardness of the political system was not just a result of retaining the habits and methods of the 1930s. Much of an earlier Russian autocratic past still influenced the political mentality of potentates accustomed to rule without much control from below. The monopoly of power, tight controls over information, an elaborate censorship system, monopoly of the media—all these trappings of absolute authority gave the leaders of the upper, and even the lower, echelons of the bureaucracy too many opportunities to abuse their offices, to misinform and lie, to conceal unfavorable news, and to wallow in unjustified luxuries.

An even deeper contradiction in the system was perceived by the intelligentsia: the newly educated population continued to be deprived of a chance to participate meaningfully in the political process. Nor was meaningful participation accorded to the party's rank and file. As a result, party members turned massively apolitical, together with the rest of the population, or sought solace and self-expression in a variety of unofficial practices and ideologies, sometimes not of the most wholesome or "progressive" kind.

This widespread political apathy expressed itself in social problems for which the ruling system had no cure to offer. New social tasks could not be addressed without the participation of all the classes of the population. Yet the system had no habit of dialogue with its citizens and could not prepare them for one. Some groups of citizens didn't really miss such dialogue and didn't demand it. Uninterested by political goings-on, they resorted to stratagems to make the best of their circumstances and to get as much as possible for the least effort.

The new line, its spokesmen confirm, realizes the gravity of the situation and the enormity of revitalizing the system. By now, one or another partial or sectoral reform will not suffice. Economic reform, for example, cannot be divorced from an understanding of the cultural sphere, of social problems, of the microforms of social life, and of the state bureaucracy. The new leaders, mostly university trained, some of them intellectually inclined, are aware of the complexity and the interdependence of the main areas of social life. Their slogans and programs show the influence of many of the ideas first proposed by social scientists.

At stake, then, is nothing less than a thorough overhaul of institutions and methods across the political spectrum. In this context, Gorbachev's use of the term *revolution* during the Twenty-seventh Party Congress seems justified. And if this revolution is to succeed, it must elicit broad support from all social strata. The support of the educated professional and intellectual classes is particularly important because of the intricacies of modern scientific, technological, administrative, and intellectual tasks. The new leadership is working to actively welcome these classes into the political process as the old regime's bureaucratic state could not: by accommodating diversity, freedom, and autonomy; by facilitating a free flow of information; and by standing ready to submit to the judgment of public opinion, whatever form it might take. The Soviet Union now has the necessary cadres capable of undertaking and participating in the renovation of the political process; indeed, it was the very presence of such layers, ready to play a leadership role, that rendered the old system so obviously inadequate.

At the same time, the working classes must also be accommodated, wooed, and, somehow, repoliticized. Without the workers' consent, interest, and participation, serious economic and political reforms cannot succeed. The old guard knew how to foment the working classes' resentment against the state's critics in the intelligentsia, but now these groups must learn to cooperate. The workers, not unlike the professional classes, will have to be convinced that the proffered political give-and-take is a serious invitation to honest bargaining, that the government is willing to listen and to compromise.

To accomplish this and inaugurate a different political game, the new leadership must vastly enlarge the political system, or, more accurately, recreate one. Previously, the state relied on state-organized formations—the trade unions, youth league, a state-guided committee for international contacts—whose political role was limited mostly to the details of the execution of policies. These few narrow social networks were not allowed to participate in a meaningful—that is, autonomous—manner in the making of policies.

The mass of party members did not fare better. The party was political only in the sense that its leaders retained political power in the state. But party members did not have a say in the process of making and executing policies; nor were there any safeguards to guarantee a role for the rank and file and the cadres in the election or rejection of party leaders. Its leadership was (and still is) a self-appointed oligarchy, though different in its make and its ways from the party of Stalin's time. Thus the party has remained an essentially administrative organization, not a political one. The task for the party today is to prove that it does express the interests and opinions of the people. Party leaders seem willing to accept this challenge in precisely such terms. Through new policies, including changes in the party's constitution, they are setting out to restore the party's legitimacy.

But the party also faces a tougher question: If there is such a mess now, who is responsible for it—and for decades of problems—if not the party? As the linchpin of the old system the party is the natural target for recriminations and accusations of all stripes. The old-style party would never address this topic. The new party leaders understand that for the public to believe the new line is real and for the party to be able to implement it, the party would have to be strongly reprimanded by its own leaders. Without such censure the public would only become incorrigibly disgusted by the hypocrisy of it all. So the party is being told to return to basic principles, to prepare for reforms, to shed its deadening stereotypes, and to become a flexible political tool ready to oversee the vast renewal and redesign of the system.

Doubtless, many in the USSR are skeptical. They have already heard many times about "democratization," about "frank talk" concerning different "woes" of daily life, about the end to "administrative methods." They are used to empty promises and insincere slogans, and they suspect that the latest bold statements from the leadership are just *ocherednoe sueslovie* ("the same verbiage again"). In this vein an embittered writer looks back to the wave of change announced in 1955: "[Since then] it has been thirty years of talking and writing about the same thing. But this is quite a timespan— more than a quarter of a century. During this time our problems managed to harden; they became familiar, intimate. We tried to solve problems according to an old scheme: by hushing up, by pushing them under the carpet, hoping that they may, suddenly, go away" [93:129].

Skepticism and cynicism are running high enough, and the new leadership knows that only a serious, credible shake-up inside the party will help win over the doubters. But to remake the party while attending to all the other tasks of the reform movement seemed almost impossible to many observers and participants. The more cautious and pragmatic leaders and cadres watched the party's first efforts at change with great uneasiness.

Not unexpectedly, the slogans and aims of reform soon aroused a growing opposition inside the party and the state apparatus, among the less well-skilled and less well-paid workers, within the conservative layers of the population at large, and among those intellectuals who

did not envisage for Russia anything but a stern authoritarianism, whether of a religious, nationalistic, or Stalinist inspiration.

It was certainly frightening for entrenched bureaucrats, used to their power and privileges, to listen to
sharp reproaches from Gorbachev and his people. The
older-style cadres, even the most honest among them,
surely felt that their world was in danger of extinction.
Swaths of officials were demoted, pensioned off, and
purged. Some foresaw the party splintering into political factions under the weight of the fancy "democratization"; the end of state authority and the monolithic
ideology would soon be followed by the downfall of the
entire system.

How can an authoritarian system allow such autonomy and submit its cherished truths to a thorough intellectual probe? For the old guard, the notion of democratization is particularly difficult to swallow. The
authoritarians know that by this term Gorbachev means
something quite different from what they themselves envisaged when they used the word. Among some of the
party leaders, the very theme of enlarging the scope of
the political process creates, according to Dobrynin, "a
good deal of consternation" [16:18].

This is a highly dramatic moment in the history of the
party. It finds itself challenged from within and from
above, by its own new leadership. Gorbachev himself
keeps repeating how serious the struggle is: "It is clear
that in the process of reorganizing our life—its renovation—a sharp, not always open, but merciless battle of
ideas, of psychological attitudes, of styles of thinking
and acting is taking place. The old does not quit without
a struggle; it finds new ways of adapting to the dynamics
of change through different scholastic and wily strata-

gems. By now, even such notions as 'acceleration' and 'reform' are being straitjacketed into obsolete dogmas and stereotypes that deprive these notions of their novel and revolutionary essence" [64:4].

The names of those leaders who oppose the new course have not yet been made public. Inertia in different groups is mentioned, but to name names would be an open declaration of war and would invite the intervention of public opinion. While disclosures may be premature, the battle against anonymous opponents is itself a token of politics in the old way: in closed chambers, in secret. Prying open internal party fights, opening them to public scrutiny, would be a triumph for democratization—the last thing the diehards want to have happen.

We can expect that as time goes on a serious coalition of forces in the party and state apparaty will become more vocal in their opposition and increase their efforts to sabotage reform. Time will show how strong the opposition is and what it can do. But if Gorbachev perseveres for two or three more years and continues to implement the changes he wants, the bells will have tolled for the old party.

11

The Political Program: A One-Party Democracy?

The strength of the opposition to Gorbachev and his policies has led certain observers to reiterate the perception that Soviet institutions—the party, the bureaucracy, the economic system—are immobile. Given this institutional rigidity, they predict an inevitable failure for the new line.

But if Soviet institutions are so inert, how could Gorbachev have risen to power in the first place? Or, for that matter, how did Khrushchev, a Stalin product par excellence, manage to inaugurate so many momentous changes? The only way one can explain how and why quite powerful reformist thrusts have repeatedly appeared inside supposedly immutable Soviet institutions is by acknowledging that over the decades many changes and transformations have occurred and accumulated within the system. (That such transformations prove to be insufficient and that institutions, such as they are, ultimately become a hindrance to national development is a different matter.) The incontrovertible fact is that the present challenge to the party and the state machinery is coming from within the powerhouse itself. These institutions, therefore, must for some time have been in the throes of serious internal mutations.

Moreover, the real story is not to be found in separate analyses of political, economic, cultural, and social phenomena. Rather we must look at the interplay of these phenomena to appreciate how radically the Soviet institutional complex as a whole has changed in the last decades. The key sectors have not evolved at the same rate. Indeed, it is because innovations in the social sphere outpaced political and economic developments that the institutions of the state came to appear relatively immobile and in need of reform.

The key lesson here is that a complicated urban society at some point stops responding to the urges of backward political institutions. The modernization of the party is therefore one of the principal aims of the new line. In our technological age, an overly controlled, heavily censored system is an aberration. Open access to information of all kinds is the indisputable precondition for the reanimation of the Soviet system.

The public clamor for a say in decisions that affect the nation's course and the public demand for the autonomy to organize in defense of their local interests and personal opinions are forcing a redefinition of the relations between the citizenry and the state. The party's claim to be the omniscient avant-garde long ago forfeited whatever credibility it had. On many crucial occasions, the party's conduct has been abysmal. Nor can the party's long-cherished assumptions and logic bear the scrutiny of Soviet intellectuals and experts. Yet without their support the party can no longer make a move.

First of all, then, the party has to become political.
Even in the absence of meaningful national elections, it
could be enough for a time if there is an active, vigilant,
and aggressive public writing letters and articles, but
also joking, gossiping, and grumbling.

In more general, structural terms, the party must acknowledge that in a contemporary urban society and
economy all the classes have a power of sorts. Every
class, therefore, must be accommodated by skillful politics, good-faith bargaining, and opportunities for economic advancement. Gorbachev has already opened
new channels to educated professionals, the fastest-
growing group in Soviet society and the most politicized, or at least among the best informed. The entry of
these professionals into the party has supplied the
cadres for the Gorbachev line, and he has responded by
asking more of them to join. The practices of glasnost
and the fostering of independent public opinion constitute broad moves to free the creative intelligentsia from
obtuse censorship and officially imposed mentors. The
government is also pledged to improve the educational
system and to enrich the scientific disciplines.

But the wish, or need, to enlarge the political system
cannot stop at welcoming into the party the professionals and intellectuals, already among the better-
provided-for classes. "Social justice," one of the cardinal
slogans, requires policies aimed at the broad population
of working people. Hence, in addition to democratizing
the party, there is talk of democratizing the workplace.
Over the last two decades a small revolution has taken
place in the relations between bosses and their subor-
dinates. The familiar and paternalistic (if not disdainful)
second-person pronoun *ty* (to which a worker responded

vy) was widely replaced by the polite, if not always respectful, use of *vy* by both parties. Of course, today the
discussion goes well beyond personal pronouns, for, as
Gorbachev is aware, his revolution must gain support
among the broad layers of the population who are still
lukewarm or hostile. Without massive pressure from below, as well as from above, the state and party bureaucracies, the ministries, and the economic enterprises
will not join in the new economic-political game.

If the party's avant-garde pretense must go, so must
the stern centralized statism that has been a fixture of
Soviet history. Statism flourished to such an extent that
the state could repeatedly contradict, in practice if not
always in rhetoric, all the basic tenets of its own official
creed. The role of the proletariat, the role of society—
everything took a backseat to what the state claimed for
itself. And the state claimed everything: it was the epit-
ome of socialism, the sole guarantor of progress, and the
principal benefactor of the nation. But, in fact, the statist
ideology was simply the rationale for an authoritarian
bureaucracy, resembling more a pathological variant of
old-fashioned nationalism than an improved version of
enlightened socialism.

The recent moves toward democratization, in turn,
raise a host of questions that will continue to be debated
in the Soviet Union and elsewhere: Can democratization
have any meaning in a one-party system? Or will continued democratization necessarily spill over to create a
multiparty system? Can one-party rule offer a meaningful outlet for political opinions and interest without destroying itself?

These are the kind of questions that make the party
stalwarts wince and accuse the reformers of undermin-

ing socialism. To many Western observers the call for democratization is either another round of the usual sham or just plain impossible in a one-party system. But the latter supposition is too negative and unimaginative. Let's consider the following.

First, if there is one sure way for Gorbachev to falter, it would be for him to look like he was weakening the party. Measures to reform the party—attacks on privileges and positions, sweeping purges, new slogans, and a modest beginning of intraparty elections—are risky enough.

But none of the reforms are intended to undermine the political preeminence of the party. It is not just a matter of concessions to hardliners. Gorbachev's wide-ranging national reforms must be supervised by a national political agency capable of leadership. Just as the reluctant state machinery must be pressured from below by an aroused citizenry, the reluctant public sectors must be pressured from above, not just by a clique of leaders, but by the whole party. Provided it learns the rules of the new political game.

Second, should the eventual turbulence produce some demands for a multiparty system, the leadership will cite national tradition and national interest to prevent an undue weakening, let alone a fragmentation, of the party. This move would garner considerable public support. For the party is the main stabilizer of the political system, and few groups would back measures likely to erode the integrity of the entire union or the centralized state. The party, especially if it refurbishes its image, is the only institution that can preside over the overhaul of the system without endangering the polity itself in the process.

Third, we must understand what the new line means by "democratization." The goal is not to install a Western-style multiparty republican system, but rather to increase citizens' participation in political life, to enhance political and other freedoms, and to return the party to a political role, instead of a basically bureaucratic-administrative one. The creation, or restoration, of a dynamic political life could offer to the masses much more than just a spectacle of democracy: an influential role for public opinion, a lively press and uninhibited electronic media, free-ranging scholarly analyses of problems of public interest, and an open political debate in the party are budding. Such practices may well give full voice to public opinion and interests. On crucial points the party could turn to the population by calling for a referendum or by allowing serious debate within the soviets and having them become a more potent political forum.

Developments like these do not happen in a week, but they are plausible illustrations of how far democratization could go and what it could mean. A historical precedent is available: the Bolshevik party, which was literally buried by Stalin and Stalinism, was a political party, with lively debates and factions. The party operated democratically, even during the civil war. It took at least eight years of struggle before the Bolshevik party was transformed into some other creature. Today, the new leadership could aim for a system of comparable political maturity. Of course, it will be a complicated process: there is considerable backwardness in the urban society; public opinion is not always enlightened or forward looking; and the broad layers of the population are particularly inexperienced, for obvious reasons, in politics.

The caution of Soviet politicians, their interest in keeping the party in one piece, is predictable. The more they enlarge the sphere of politics, elicit and receive autonomous initiatives, allow and encourage nonsponsored organizations and groups, the more turbulence they should expect. As a reign of terror is not feasible and would be, in any case, irrelevant in such a situation, we may see a one-party system that learns to live in a society where many things happen outside the party's control and where the party's policies are routinely tested by the population, sometimes in dramatic confrontations.

This is not a picture that a *derzhimorda* ("a police bully") would look forward to, but the scenario is conceivable. It would be the upshot of the democratization that seems to be the aim of the Gorbachev leadership.

12

The Economic Hurdle:
Planning and Markets

The economy has played a relatively small role in our presentation thus far. We have concentrated on the changes in the social environment, which, of course, reflected economic facts, industrialization policies, and methods of economic management. But now we may turn to the economy proper. It is in bad shape, as is now often heard in the USSR, because of a faulty "economic mechanism." Ever since the economic reforms proclaimed in 1965 were abandoned, the performance of the economy has continuously worsened. The rates of growth have continued to fall, and the quality of the output has deteriorated. Further, some of the growth in the national income was based on a boost in low-quality output. The rising quantity of poorly made goods looked like growth, but often ended up as unnecessary and unsalable inventory. Some enterprises worked *na sklad*— "for the storehouse"—more than for their customers and still earned their salaries, wages, and even bonuses [2:3].

When the Central Committee recently examined this

alarming situation (where were they before?), their first prescription was that from now on the enterprises had to earn their salaries and wages, had to cover their costs and show profits. This dictum, of course, meant that the entire economic system had to be reshaped.

The issues of economic reform are certainly no less intractable than those of political reform. But there is a key difference: the political dangers of not instituting reforms in the economy are likely to exceed the political dangers of pressing forward with changes. The impression is that the leadership is seeking reforms of political and other institutions, improvement of the overall popular mood and of the social climate, because those are seen as preconditions for a successful reshaping of the economic model, the most difficult task of all.

Special committees are working to devise a new economic model, and the heated public debates are probably matched by even more passionate behind-the-scenes skirmishing. Among the scholars, a variety of remedies, most first proposed in the 1960s, are being offered in print. The consensus calls for the bulk of enterprises to operate by the principle of *samookupaemost'* (production must recover costs) and the related idea of *samofinansirovanie* (producers must finance their activities without government bailouts).

As with the political system, some observers insist that the Soviet economy is not reformable, that certain models of planning, managing, and producing are immobile. Again, our thesis is that the actual economy—which is, of course, more complicated than any model—is, by now, more flexible and amenable to reforms than is often realized. The system is not a monolith: there is a give-and-take between agencies and factories; there are differences in approach and attitude between the ministerial bureaucrats and the actual producers; and certain big branches, or even enterprises, can impose on the government lower planning targets and higher prices for their products. (These privileged monopolists are not unlike some powerful Western corporations.)

We also know that factory managers have developed a vast repertoire of methods to handle the rigid government plans they receive, to defend themselves against unrealistic targets, to look good and get paid, and to make the system work sometimes despite itself. They know what salaries, wages, bonuses, and prices are, who wields what power, and how to cope within the system. Hoarding spare labor and other resources, concealing reserves, wheeling and dealing directly with other managers to obtain supplies that the official supply network is not delivering, selling and buying many millions of rubles worth of excess equipment—all these practices, some illicit and some tolerated, are part of the real economic world. Some other model exists only on paper.

In sum, Soviet managers react and adapt, as best they can, to the parameters imposed on them. If those parameters define a situation of rising investments and falling rates of growth and quality, the system has but itself to blame. Given other parameters, the same managers or, if necessary, their replacements will learn how to work within those, too. The state, if it is resolute enough, can change the parameters and thus remake the economic environment to suit its broader goals.

Moreover, in its departures from the paper model, the real economy has a lot to offer in the way of suggestions for an alternative model. Were this not the case, any reform would be unthinkable. The system as it operates clearly contains more than just elements of a quasi-market mechanism playing only third fiddle to the model in place. Rather, the real economy functions according to two complementary but also contradictory logics: the logic of the ownership system and the logic of economic reality.

The productive apparatus, as we have seen, is used to some level of improvisation and spontaneity. Initial resistance to economic reform is more likely to come from the ministerial bureaucracy. The economic ministries, we must recall, did not evolve organically from economic activities. They were superimposed as a separate, upper layer on the producers to administer an economic expansion based on the fulfillment of production targets and the raising of targets once the old ones were attained. But the remuneration of the ministries' staffs did not depend on the performance of the economy. The result was a network of overgrown and powerful central bureaucracies overseeing an ineffective, inefficient economic organism of low productivity. Reformist thinkers have long sought to reduce the ministries' power, to transform them from purely administrative into coordinating agencies, and to link their bonuses to measures of economic activity.

Under the ministries' supervision and multitarget plans, the enterprises managed to produce poor or useless goods, showed little interest in complicated and cumbersome renovations, and opted for as convenient a routine as possible. The economic system was geared to satisfy the supervisory bureaucracy, not customers or consumers, even as it guaranteed enterprises against losses and bankruptcy. Interestingly, when the bureaucracy was itself the direct consumer and expected the merchandise to meet specifications, quality was noticeably higher [108:55–56]. The Soviet military, for example, was able to procure what it wanted, and the armament industries are known for quality output, including products destined for the civilian economy.

If indeed the purchaser's insistence on quality affects the standards of production, then the new economic environment must give power to consumers and allow them to exercise strong pressure on producers. It is well in the range of Soviet means to authorize strong, autonomous organizations of consumers, endowed with access to administrations, the press, and the courts. The reformers are also searching for ways to introduce more powerful competitive elements that would help keep producers on their toes, alert to interesting technological innovations and more aware of costs.

A full-blown free-market system, however, would be ideologically unacceptable to Soviet leaders and probably to the public. But it is worth noting that in modern Western economies the free market is a ghost of the past. In such economies three sectors are the main players in the economic game: the state, the corporations, and the mass of smaller agents. The game is regulated by the state, through legislation, taxation, and direct investments, notably in research. Although the powerful corporations are hostile to state meddling, massive state intervention is a cornerstone of every modern Western economy, and the corporations gladly accept government bailouts, encourage the state to conduct or pay for much of the needed research, and benefit from having their executives and most employees trained for them at the expense, primarily, of the state.

In any case, though the corporations operate in markets, their economic power, access to credits, control over suppliers, and international mobility enable them to shape, not just follow, the rules of the economic game. By contrast, the third sector, small-scale companies, is truly a market sector in which firms scramble to compete according to the rules established by the state and the corporations. It is an important but unequal player.

In the Soviet case, if one excludes the black markets, there are only two sectors: the state and its economic organizations. The latter have a certain independence, despite being fully state-owned, and can be seen as the equivalents of corporations that can and do collaborate with the state, in different ways, everywhere. But the third sector, as a serious partner, is missing. Its introduction is on the reformers' agenda, too, not just for the sake of consumer interest but also in order to make price, a key element of market mechanisms, an important factor in the performance of all players. A market sector will also stimulate competition.

The value of small firms is better understood by Soviet economists and policy makers now that the intoxication with bigness per se has ended. They have not failed to notice the creative role smaller entrepreneurs have played in modern technological fields in the West. No doubt, smaller firms are going to be encouraged, without necessarily creating a capitalist class ready to take over the economy. The small operators could include cooperatives, state organizations serving as subcontractors for bigger firms or for the government, and new entrants into the private sector about to be legalized.

The emerging strategy to pressure Soviet producers to shape up includes both such a renascent internal private sector and the presence of foreign investors, who would independently manage firms, even if co-owned by the state. Competition from smaller firms, from foreign investor-managers and, more broadly, from a deeper involvement in world markets all would contribute to the sought-after reform of the economic system.

In this revitalized market, Soviet firms would be asked to succeed financially without straying entirely from the requirements of broader national interests. For there is no wish in the leadership, nor among the economists, to scrap centralized economic planning. Planning, the argument runs, failed because it was part and parcel of a faulty economic model and because the planners sought to supervise every detail of every branch. The new goal is to turn planning into a parameter-setting activity rather than a target-setting exercise, that will work through the pricing system and will attend to long-term and broad national issues; for example, the proportions and intersectoral relations in the economy and the pace of scientific and technological advances. All the rest will be left to other economic agencies, such as the fiscal authorities, and to spontaneity.

There is also some talk about more autonomy for workers in the workplace, a bigger say in management and greater involvement in the reforms. This is not anything revolutionary; indeed, it could have come from an editorial in the *New York Times* that sums up the "obvious remedies" for inefficiencies in American business: "trim costs, thin executive staff, invite wider employee participation in planning and operation, spend more on research" [75:18].

No simple formulas like "employee participation" can hint at the tasks facing the Soviet leadership. Boldness on the part of the leadership is necessary, but a nation's political will does not depend on the courage of a few leaders. We cannot at this moment judge the will of the broader circles of policy makers who will be asked to vote nor of the more numerous, but equally important, administrators who will be asked to execute the complicated changes. It is too soon to tell whether the highest-ranking leaders will be able to convince the intermediary people of the gravity of the situation and the heavy price of failing to take bold action. Obviously, the reforms were launched. Will the apparaty persevere?

This is why the leadership is also taking the argument beyond the administrations, straight to the public. The social contours of an alliance committed to major economic reform are taking shape before our eyes. For the creative intelligentsia in the arts and the sciences, the new line opens new horizons, not to mention opportunities for prestige and influence. Economic reform has many supporters among the social scientists, some of whom were the theoretical and ideological pioneers of the new line. And the most able, creative, and talented engineers as well as technicians from many echelons in the hierarchy have long been frustrated by the rusty economic mechanisms and by bureaucratic inefficiencies. One would expect similar support for reform from the better-skilled workers, who have no reason to fear "intensification."

Numerous studies of high school–educated young workers, who constitute a large proportion of the newcomers in the labor force, show them, too, to be quite frustrated by the inadequacies and primitive conditions of the workplace. Reforms aimed at raising professional standards and eliminating the proverbial disequilibria, one of them being the underutilized educational and professional potential of labor, should appeal to them. The young in the factories and elsewhere can also find in the reformist line an attempt to resolve the contradictions and discrepancies between the ethos and values they learned in school and the economic, political, and social realities of everyday life. The promises of reform open a broad outlet for renewed youthful idealism, a valuable commodity still in short supply.

Among a variety of social groups, then, there would seem to be some support for comprehensive economic reforms. In the absence of opinion polls, we cannot know how strong that support might be. But it appears likely that in all the key sectors there are enough pioneering trend setters to convince their cohorts to seriously consider the arguments in favor of reform.

Conclusion

As we have seen, in the past thirty years the Soviet Union has reached a new stage in its development. It has become predominantly urban, and although national and regional traditions still weigh heavily in many ways, the social structure is a new one. For the first time in Russian history, the state system is presiding over a society quite different from the one the tsars or Lenin and Stalin knew. Nonetheless, the state system itself—despite numerous, sometimes far-reaching changes undertaken to meet the imperatives of the new times—still clung to strong vestiges of an age-old agrarian despotism. The institutions and methods of state building inherited from Stalin were a product of a rural country steeped in the authoritarian tradition that Stalin "perfected" to a monstrous degree.

Although considerably reformed and strongly diluted, the anachronistic autocratic features have now come under pressure from the social environment. The apparaty, not too alert to the call of history, has been reminded that the muzhik (the implicit, sometimes explicit justification for the crude dictatorial regime) is no longer at center stage. Today well-educated urban citizens, not backward peasants, are the largest demographic group.

The new urban reality emerged quite quickly, and the

resulting compression of historical stages manifested itself in superimposed layers of social development. Thus
the habits and mind-set of rural culture, brought into the
cities by millions of migrants, coexisted with stages of
development characteristic of two earlier industrial
eras, and simultaneously with the ethos and culture of
the modern scientific and technological age. (The sociological x-ray of three generations presented in chapter 3
is a good illustration of coexisting layers of social development.) The interplay of these different social structures and cultures makes the emerging urban society a
very complicated one. It is still in transition, still
evolving.

In the meantime, the dimensions and potential of this
novel society, especially its political aspects, are still
poorly understood. But one thing is clear: Soviet society
needs a state that can match its complexity. And in ways
sometimes overt, sometimes covert, contemporary urban society has become a powerful "system maker,"
pressuring both political institutions and the economic
model to adapt. Through numerous channels, some visible, some slow, insidious, and imperceptible, Soviet urban society is affecting individuals, groups, institutions,
and the state. Civil society is talking, gossiping, demanding, sulking, expressing its interests in many ways
and thereby creating moods, ideologies, and public
opinion. At the same time, the impersonal, structural
features of the social system create hard facts, define
reality, and set limits. Both the personal and impersonal
factors disregard controlling devices such as censorship,
police controls or the *nomenklatura* (nomination process). As we have seen, when politicians are inattentive,
they soon reach a dead end.

Although everyone is now trying to predict how Gorbachev's reforms will fare, the principal historical lesson before us is to fully appreciate the radical and irreversible changes that have already taken place. The structural changes in the economy and society proceeded independently of policies and politics. Since the 1950s the country has continued to become increasingly urbanized, educated, professionally differentiated, and politically, ideologically, and culturally diversified. The political façade of monolithic uniformity can no longer be taken seriously by anyone. Complex urban networks shape individuals, filter official views, and create an infinite welter of spontaneities. Baffled, the conservative leaders were left with the choice of trying to control the uncontrollable or disregarding, and thereby mishandling, the spontaneous. Either recourse would inevitably produce great downturns and put the entire state system under crippling pressure.

The coalescence of a civil society capable of extracurricular action and opinion making, independent of the wishes of the state, marks the start of a new age, from which there is no turning back. A massive public is ready to listen to different, controversial voices, not only those from the realm of the arts. The samizdats are more numerous and diverse than we realize.

More broadly, during the preceding thirty years, a period unscarred by Stalinist-style repression and characterized by slower rates of growth, urban society, though not yet entirely settled (if it ever can be), has been able to solidify. A huge class of educated specialists has emerged, and different elites, previously so heavily brutalized, have had time to recreate themselves or to recover. Or, at least, an educated pool of talent from which elites can be quickly composed and recomposed, is now at hand.

The size, responsibilities, and effectiveness of the new elites is a crucial topic. Under Stalin's oligarchic rule, a small group of top officials possessed the plenitude of power, privilege, and status. But even then, a broad layer of far-less-powerful elites was needed to run the system. The power accorded those on the lower rungs was "on loan," as it were, or ceded by default because the lords of the immense manor could not be everywhere and see everything. In the absence of meaningful links with influential networks in society at large, these elites ruled in an almost conspiratorial manner, in secrecy. After Stalin's death, the scope of the elites was enlarged and something like a "political class," a body that participated in the making of some policies, emerged.

Today, the elites are even more ramified: the indispensable lower rungs are broader, more competent, and more influential. Their importance is not just "reflected" or "borrowed," but grounded in a relative independence and tenure. Abutting the bureaucratic upper layers are networks of social elites that have ascended by force of their own achievement: the upper tiers of scholars, artists, technicians, social thinkers, and some administrators and bureaucrats whose prestige was acquired by merit, not rank. There is no doubt that the old narrow elite networks, the almost secret oligarchy, have been breached.

If we knew more about these new elites, we would have an excellent measure for assessing more precisely the prospects and the character of the reforms. Serious democratization, even *à la russe*, requires a complex leadership structure that branches out into the social maze on all levels and communicates with all rungs on the ladder. Today, the necessary prospective cadres are available and appear, even if hesitant, ready to step into the fray. The emergence of a reform-minded and educated leadership inside the party and inside the bureaucracies is a result of the same process. Facing them, inside but mostly outside the party and the bureaucracies, is a large constituency, a mass of people of different ages, ready to join the political process and back the leadership. We do not know how many, inside and outside the power structure, are ready to join *against* this leadership. But if Gorbachev and his allies can maintain their current course and incorporate into the political process groups close to them in outlook, they will in the coming years conquer the party from below. The battle for entry into the new age, now unfolding before our eyes, could then be won.

As we turn to the question of what the future holds, we begin with two caveats. First, all our observations and hypotheses about what is taking place in the Soviet Union must be predicated on an understanding of that nation as a historical entity, replete with social and political complexities and transformations. To ignore thirty-five years of development since Stalin's death, to obtusely repeat, as some still do, that "nothing ever changes over there" is a bit of foolishness that neither scholars nor policy makers can afford.

Second, too many important features of the system are too little known to us and unpredictable to the leaders themselves. We don't know enough about the bureaucracy or the working classes and their perceptions of what is at stake. We also are in the dark about the party apparatus and the party as a whole. Up to now rank-and-file party members have had no important role to play. Who can imagine what this hitherto mute mass might say if given a voice? Thus far public debates have revealed inside the party an unexpectedly strong pro-reform constituency. And there are historical precedents for supposedly well-controlled dummy parties suddenly changing their skin.

A short story, "Levers" (*rychagi*), written by Aleksandr Iashin in 1956, nicely illustrates how formal structures affect people's political "personalities." A group of kolkhoz members are conversing freely about solutions to a broad range of critical problems facing their kolkhoz. Suddenly the tone changes: one of them has opened the session of their party cell. The frank, clear, and honest conversation is replaced by the deadwood of official verbiage. Once the workers assume their function as cogs in the official machine, they adopt the persona of automatons. Today, the Soviet leadership seems to be counting on the new freedoms to release pent-up social energy and creativity within the party. It was that hidden energy that produced Gorbachev, and now he must continue to mine that vein.

Proponents of strict authoritarian methods of rule, however, are not in short supply. They come from nationalist and other conservative traditions; some are neo-Stalinists. Although they are still powerful, they have already had their chances and failed. In some countries authoritarian, even backward, political systems have successfully modernized their economies; notably, in different ways, Imperial Germany, Imperial Japan, Imperial Russia, and the USSR itself, to a point. But, for very good reasons, the current Soviet leadership is persuaded that the country's modernization now depends on a democratization of the one-party system. No one, we repeat, is urging a Western-style multiparty democracy. But plans are afoot to narrow the sphere of the state, to broaden meaningful political participation, and to encourage a robust civil society.

A democratized one-party system is a distinct possibility, at least as a phase in development. As an original historical phenomenon, this system would have its distinct national peculiarities and would continue to evolve under pressure from the social system.* These adaptations and readaptations, their nature or timing, are not predictable, for the laws of development do not follow any timetable.

In the meantime, the USSR is entering its new age and trying to recover what it missed or mishandled in previous stages, for example, the bourgeois-democratic revolution of March 1917 and the socialist promises of the October Revolution. The conditions may now be ripe or ripening for the system to reclaim some of the hopes of its idealistic revolutions.

"Shedding stereotypes" is a revealing, liberating, and militant aspect of the current policy. Among the stereotypes sent to the dustbin by proponents of the new orientation is the old practice of relegating improvements in the system to some hypothetical and incredible (actually quite ridiculous) "first and second stages of communism." This chimera produced a dreary but endless literature and some of the most deadening courses in schools and universities.

---

*Such pressures will certainly work against any party monopoly on power and they are already growing, in view of the fact that Grobachev did not manage so far to transform the party into a credible, renovated, political organization. He himself is actually broaching the idea of a multi-party system, notably in order to spur the party into internal reform. My reflection about a temporary "one-part democracy" was predicated on such a transformation. The other alternative is for the party to simply be wiped out, with or without elections. [M.L., January 1990]

Gone, too, is the sterile "bureaucratic utopia" in which society was to become ever more homogeneous as communism advanced. The new leadership understands the heterogeneity of today's society and economy, and it realizes that an acceptance of diversity in social and economic forms is prerequisite to reforming the state, "socializing" the state, as it were, and drawing society into politics, or "politicizing" society. Politicians and experts agree that the state sectors, central and local, should be flanked by strong cooperative sectors, private family enterprises, and foreign-owned or co-owned businesses; that the market mechanism should have a growing role; that a multilayered economy must be allowed to evolve as it will.

This means that a very different political game is in the making and is already, to some extent, practiced. Authoritarian coercion, once a favored tool, would no longer be of much use. Instead internal politics is learning to use a new language: interplay and bargaining, yielding and conforming, pressuring and compromising, giving and taking. In brief, *real* politics, negotiations among groups and classes that are coming into their own as autonomous partners in the new game. It is a new authoritarianism of a quite different type, still *à la russe*, but after all, most regimes in history have been authoritarian.

In an earlier book, I depicted the Soviet historical drama as a two-act play repeated several times with different sets and casts [61:123–24, 355]. And I asked whether Soviet history had only two prototypes—"war communism" and the NEP—from which to choose. The answer to this question seems to be at hand. Beginning in the 1960s, a new trend in Soviet political and intellectual life surfaced in the debates about economic reforms. The country was shown a way to overcome the crippling consequences of the civil-war model, "to drop the unrealistic monolithic cant and to develop the regime in a direction that will allow Soviet society to enter an age of political reason, escaping for good the seemingly fatal bi-model pendulum."

More than twenty years later, Soviet Russia is at it again, trying. There is no dearth of programs and remedies for change, and there are no insurmountable barriers to it. The nation has continued to evolve, and will continue to do so. But for a comprehensive reform program to be enacted sooner, rather than later and in worse conditions, political will is necessary. The will is now there, and one of the most remarkable stories of our time is now unfolding.

Part
Three

The End of the Gorbachev
Phenomenon?

13

Perestroika:
The Genie Out of the Bottle

When I wrote Parts One and Two of this book, in February 1987, I was not attempting to forecast all the possible effects of perestroika, but rather to explain its essence and to hint at its potential. So much has happened since then that it seems worthwhile to reexamine the premises of my arguments in light of recent events.

In a nutshell, my analysis of the Soviet reform movement ran as follows:

Over the years, and especially since the 1960s, a civil society began to emerge in the USSR, in the midst of a statist system that should not have had one. As this civil society took root, it instigated changes "from below," in the social, economic, and political structures of the country. Slowly and haltingly at first, the economic system, mostly the product of the 1930s, reached its limits and began literally to bankrupt the country. The Soviet political system, deeply enmeshed in the economic system and structured so as to exclude citizens from political participation, was incapable of accommodating the new social reality and the corresponding new attitudes of the citizenry.

The political system was at the end of its tether: turbulence, crisis, and, eventually, reform were inevitable. When all three finally came, they were launched "from above," by the party leadership. This startled some observers—yet, in truth, it should not have. Previous reform efforts had also come from the party, indicating that this organization, through some of its cadres and leaders, understood the deep changes that the country was experiencing as a result of decades of poorly managed, or unmanaged, urbanization.

The subsequent wave of reforms, however, did not necessarily have to lead to democracy; not every urban or urbanizing society necessarily turns democratic. But it stood to reason that democratization might ensue because of the character and national circumstances of the Soviet crisis. The culprit here was a severely authoritarian and disciplinarian system, now obviously discredited. On the political level, the solution consisted of repoliticizing the system, of involving civil society—the great new, powerful presence—in the political process. From there it was only a single step, however difficult, for civil society to actually run the country. Democracy was thus firmly placed on the Russian historical agenda, and the appearance of Gorbachev and his program responded to the challenge. Hence the "Gorbachev phenomenon."

This analytic approach has proven very fruitful. Tracking the long-term historical trends that shape current events, without entering into fast-moving particulars, enables us to uncover the roots of the current crisis and to clarify the historical agenda that the Soviet system has had to address. Despite all the uncertainties—

more accurately, an entire system of uncertainties—inherent in the Soviet situation, I believe that my analysis continues to explain the key features of the unfolding Soviet drama. Events in the Soviet Union (and in Eastern Europe, for that matter) are proceeding at a feverish pace, and yet I would argue that although new acts and scenes have been written, the play is still the same. Naturally, no one can predict the final shape of things to come; yet within the evenemental flux we can discern emerging phenomena and new features that portend the future.

Though I have remained confident in my method, at some moments the roller-coaster quality of Gorbachev's career tempted me to delete his name from the title of this book. First, Gorbachev was seen as a charismatic international star. Then, people began talking about a faltering leader beset by interminable dangers and failures. There has been no other politician in our times whose fall has been so insistently and repeatedly predicted. Yet Gorbachev remains at the helm, and the democratizing orientation of his political program remains on course, despite the twists, compromises, and slowdowns that irritate his critics and worry his supporters.

Moreover, whatever may happen to Gorbachev, there is obviously a Gorbachev phenomenon independent of the man himself. The political essence of the Gorbachev phenomenon—the repoliticizing of the political system—continues unabated. The one-party system has been shattered, the new-style presidency has been approved, and Gorbachev's intention to eliminate altogether the office of party general secretary might have left the country—whether it is still the USSR or just Russia—with one democratically elected official, the

president, in charge. Although the title of General Secretary was not abolished, the party and its ruling structure are in fact losing their previous grip on the state,
and the result is actually the same.

No one doubts that outstanding leadership at the
right moment can be absolutely critical for a nation's
destiny. Gorbachev is there just at this kind of moment,
although the impact of his leadership cannot yet be fully
assessed. His career has been punctuated by spectacular
ups and downs but, even if he is weakening, some say
fading away, the political and social reforms are even
more profound than originally intended.

The civil society that was emerging in 1987 is now
highly visible, with hundreds of thousands of informal,
independent groups of all types, including an array of
political ones. The insatiable quest for information and
for open debate on all issues has exceeded all expectations for glasnost. Topics treated with the greatest caution and self-censorship only yesterday are now openly
and sharply discussed in the national press and in literature of all genres. Stalin's crimes, the abuses committed by the Soviet security forces and police, the entire political process and all its personalities—almost all
the old taboos have been suspended. Today, the press is
an influential educator of people, though occasionally
also a source of bewilderment and disorientation to
readers suddenly asked to absorb an unprecedented
stream of information about their nation's problems.

Having launched glasnost and perestroika in the
name of the party, Gorbachev at first hoped that by democratizing the party from within he could control the
incipient political pluralism and prolong the party's influence and power. During that early phase of perestroika, there was no interest in rushing to a multiparty

system; there were no credible forces to even seriously demand it. Today, however, a multiparty system is not only *on* the agenda, it *is* the agenda, and Gorbachev's acceptance of political pluralism signaled the seriousness of his reformist orientation. Even so, it has undermined much of his initial mass support, notably because of the weakening of the party.

The party, of course, is still in power, but it lives on borrowed time and is already quite a different creature. Despite a number of retreats and periods of annoying procrastination, Gorbachev has continued to considerably weaken the old party system, and he has rather doggedly pursued the objective of creating a renovated state capable of succeeding the party as a seat of power and sovereignty.

Moreover, the party is undergoing a spontaneous process of change, independent of anyone's wishes. Though the party as an administrative grid was incapable of serving as a real political organization, from its ranks have come veritable political leaders. The revival of political life has deeply penetrated the membership, and the political battles and cleavages that have appeared in the electorate at large have also divided the party membership and all layers of the party apparatus and leadership. The depth of this internal differentiation is hard to gauge, but a seemingly irreversible step was taken when the Parliament amended the Constitution and abolished the party's monopoly on power. It is very doubtful that any future Soviet congress could, even if it wanted to, reinstate a one-party monopoly.

The party has had enormous difficulty in accepting its fate as only one of the voices in a pluralist system, as an entity that must relinquish power at the will of the electorate. Whether gropingly or by design, the outflanking of the party through electoral procedures has begun, and the final test for the party is nearing. In election after election, conservative and reformist party members have been fighting it out among themselves. More important than the results of any particular election, though, is the spontaneous sociological and political process already at work: political differentiation of the membership, splits and coalitions, and simple dissolution are all realistic prospects. The party is already split in many ways, and not just into factions but potentially into different parties.

The next step, and one of Gorbachev's officially declared objectives, is to make the party relinquish its economic and administrative functions in order to transform itself from a bureaucratic ruling machine into a political party. The party will therefore have to descend into the political arena, without its police safeguards or economic privileges, to face the pluralist society that Gorbachev and his people have acknowledged.

The party's leading reformers, though, have lost some of their early buoyancy. After an easy-looking start, the reforms became dangerously bogged down, especially the economic measures. The early slogan *uskorenie* ("acceleration," referring to economic development) is not heard anymore. The social reforms—the optimistic "orientation on the social sphere," once so confidently proclaimed—have been placed on the back burner: the economy cannot yet finance new social services or improvements in living conditions. Another reform, the anti-alcohol campaign, was too rushed and had to be abandoned.

It is now clear that the reason for the slowdown was that the political equation was not yet ready for a new regime to emerge and deepen the entire perestroika.

Gorbachev had no choice but to apply the brakes. The intermittent halts momentarily renewed the hopes of his opponents but, to their dismay, Gorbachev has been able to continue moving forward even with the brakes applied.

For now no one can say what was included in Gorbachev's original blueprint and what he improvised in response to unfolding events. His policies opened the floodgates and, for a time, it appeared as though he was being overtaken and engulfed by the floods. That the entire system did not collapse must be attributed to the intellectual and political readiness of Gorbachev and his supporters to accept the consequences of their initial breakthrough. Moreover, they were able to some extent to control potentially explosive pressures, including the extreme nationalisms, by preserving, for a transitional period, the more vital and useful structures of the old system.

The interim maneuvering was not without costs. The more impatient reformers accused Gorbachev of treason, or at least foot-dragging, while the conservative groups, with whom Gorbachev compromised for a time, circulated their own fears and suspicions. But Gorbachev's compromising posture goes a long way toward explaining why Russia has not seen an overnight expulsion of the powerholders of the old regime, has not suffered a Rumanian- or Czechoslovakian-style sweep.

Many of the more radical reformers have been quietly biding their time, but not Boris Eltsin, the erstwhile fervent proponent of social justice in the Politbureau. Eltsin was evicted by Gorbachev and began to look like a competitor, even a credible one, according to some. A product of one of Gorbachev's errors, Eltsin has become somewhat of a phenomenon himself. As president of the

Russian republic, he could provoke serious new trouble for Gorbachev. Despite Eltsin's penchant for populist demagoguery and his act of quitting the party, he too may still in the end have to make compromises with his arch-rival.

The disappointments expressed by some sectors of the intelligentsia, the outbursts of nationalist aspirations, the difficulties of enacting reform have transformed the political game into a much more complicated and risky affair, into a real gamble. Thus far Gorbachev has turned out to be a masterful player, surmounting cumulative adversities that would have finished off a lesser figure several times over. But the reform of the economy, as almost everyone is saying, cannot wait any longer. A system cannot exist without an economy—a statement so true it is almost trite. If nothing is done, the economic crisis will deepen, precipitating a frightening ruin. If the proper reforms are instituted, the crisis will deepen for a time, but eventually a working economy may arise.

Just as politics has been reentering the polity, so too economics must reenter the economy. In this sense, the economic system inherited by Gorbachev was both archaic and unnatural, wholly incompatible with historically proven patterns of modern economic life. It was, to a large extent, an emergency system that had no future, a system that was bankrupting the nation and had to be replaced.

All too hesitatingly, legislation is moving in the right direction, toward a multisectoral economy that has roles for both the market and the state. Although formidable, the difficulties of switching to a multisectoral system should not be exaggerated. Once the minimal avenues are open for economic activity—in terms of legislation, incentives, and the recasting of the administrative grid—private, group, and organizational (corporate) initiatives will begin to avail themselves of those avenues. The nation's economic needs are strong, and as soon as the first positive signs of change begin to be felt, various initiatives will necessarily be forthcoming and the pace of economic restructuring will accelerate.

Regarding the role of the state in the new economy, little need be said: As in most successful economies of our day, the state will have an important role. A more complicated affair is the fate of the idea of socialism. Very briefly, we may note that "free markets," as the current slogan goes, are not the only component of economic systems and are therefore never really free: economies are always mixed. Other components—initiatives and autonomy, local and central institutions—control and correct the effects of economic spontaneities. More broadly, the ways in which societal interests are realized in economic life are of the utmost importance. (Here is where ideology comes in.) Thus it is the interplay of various components of the economy, the state, and the society, as well as the relative weight of each that together determine whether a system is or becomes capitalist, socialist, or something else. At the moment, how the USSR will navigate among these broad alternatives is still very much in doubt.

For now, though, attention continues to be focused on the empty grocery shelves—a painfully miserable sight and deeply compromising for the government—and on the nationalist stirrings and the quest for independence among some of them. The latter is often depicted as *the crisis*, perhaps the fatal blow to perestroika.

The trouble is very deep, but the epicenter of it is Russia, not the nationalities. The survival of the USSR depends on the Russian and Ukrainian republics. If the Russian republic begins to tackle its problems and if relations with the Ukraine survive the current factionalism, the USSR will survive, in a new constitutional arrangement, and remain a superpower. The problems of the other nationalities will in retrospect be seen as symptoms, not as the core of the Soviet Union's trouble. I do not mean to suggest that nationalism is unimportant, only that Russian nationalism will be more crucial to the shaping of the nation's future than, say, demands for independence in Azerbaijan.

But if Russia does not soon begin to solve some of its most urgent problems, the USSR will cease to exist and Russia itself will become a second-rate, poorly developed, and probably not truly independent country. This menacing perspective frightens some Russians into immobility, but spurs the best forces into action. They realize that their fate depends not upon how many republics remain in a transformed USSR but on the readiness and ability of those that remain to seriously reform and, notably, to begin to populate and develop Siberia. This, of course, is not a short-term project, but it is the real project.

Such ideas should have been understood by many Russians, but, contrary to the expectations of Gorbachev and his allies, there has been no widespread popular call for a serious consolidation of forces in order to effect the salvation of the country and the preservation of its newly acquired freedoms.

Indeed, the political freedoms and economic reforms are being fought tooth-and-nail by many members of the vast sociopolitical structure who profited from the *zastoi* ("stagnation") and have a vested interest in maintaining the status quo. Opponents of perestroika include not only bureaucrats but also unknown proportions of workers and poorer and less-educated people as well as those citizens who have become psychologically dependent on strong power figures. Opponents to perestroika are also, of course, to be found inside the security apparatus and among intellectuals; indeed, intellectuals can be found in leadership roles in all the main currents that have recently emerged in Soviet political life.

Among these groups are the lukewarm reformers who prefer dealing with the economy first and politics later; the solid technocrats, who are neither nationalistic nor ideologically conservative; and various nationally minded—but not excessively nationalistic—groups that show varying degrees of interest in and support for reform. Given the scope and complexity of the issues, there is room for enormous diversity: a free-market economy or not? an intact USSR or several states linked constitutionally or otherwise? a Western-style democracy? a Western-style economy *and* a Western-style polity? back to authoritarianism? The combinations of answers to these questions alone could create a dozen contending parties.*

There is also quite a lot of pessimism and despondency, demoralization and despair, which a new regime must overcome if it is to consolidate its power. Otherwise, the people's deep "moral vacuum" (the term recently used by Soviet sociologists L. A. Gordon and E. V. Klopov) will render any system ineffective.

In the meantime, in the wake of Gorbachev's initiatives, the international scene has been transformed quite

*Julietto Chiesa, the highly competent Moscow correspondent for the Italian newspaper *Unita*, conducted a painstaking study of the Soviet Parliament and discerned seven political families among its deputies. I thank him for sharing his unpublished research with me.

deeply, notably in Eastern and Central Europe, and with amazing speed. The speed, incidentally, can be explained by reference to the erosion of their systems, similar in many ways to that taking place in the USSR itself. As a result of this erosion, these crisis-laden countries were craving change, and some were better prepared for it than the USSR.*

The close of the 1980s witnessed the virtual end of the cold war, the end of the Stalinist empire, and an emerging new configuration of power in Western Europe—indeed, in the Western world in general. The Council for Mutual Economic Assistance (COMECON) is almost extinct, and Germany has suddenly begun to loom very large on the European and world horizon. The specter of German domination has caused some to worry about the future of the European Community, while others forecast that the European Community will, on the contrary, so thrive as to dethrone the United States from its preeminent position in Europe. The eclipse of the United States as a European power, in turn, will further thwart U.S. efforts to retain the leading superpower status that the cold war afforded it. Russia, quite obviously, has already entered a period of decline, as has the star of Gorbachev, even if he remains in power.

The cascade of international events triggered by Gorbachev's policies seems to have swamped and diminished him, especially when the internal situation in Russia became, to say the least, stuck midcourse. But other, more favorable twists are also on the horizon. Very close ties between Germany and Russia (or what remains of the USSR), especially economic ties, may in the near fu-

---

*I have discussed the international repercussions of perestroika in "Perestroika—a New Historical Stage," *Journal of International Affairs* 42, no. 2 (Spring 1989).

ture be very helpful to the latter. Broader cooperation between the USSR and Europe is another possibility, as is increased international competition between Europe, Japan, and the United States for access to the potentially fabulous Russian markets.

While these political and economic realignments proceed, one hears in the media, and in intellectual circles as well, talk of "the end of ideology" or, in the newer jargon, "the end of history," a vacuous slogan that has gained currency for some mysterious reason. Both phrases imply that there was only one ideology—the communist one—and that with its disintegration, the era of an unideological universe (basically a conservative "free market" world?) has dawned. What the sloganeers seem to ignore is that, in truth, ours is an era of ever more distorted and fragile market economies desperately in need of a new configuration between the social, economic, and political spheres.

Analyses of current Soviet affairs also founder on two types of bias that magnify the severity of an admittedly severe situation. One source of distortion arises from observers misinterpreting the fears and gloomy predictions expressed by Soviet citizens. The Soviets are a people genuinely overwhelmed, and strained, by the unprecedented novelty of daily events. Their initial euphoria and exhilaration have been dampened by revelations of their country's long-hidden problems and ailments. Inevitably, these revelations have produced a pervading sense of fragmentation; people can no longer mouth the pretense of the old ruling ideology, the pat assurance that "all is in order." Ideologies and value systems already seriously eroded before glasnost have now crumbled completely. Of course, glasnost did not produce this crisis—it merely brought it into the limelight and sharpened the popular perception of the disarray into which the old unifying themes had fallen.

Much of what looks like social fragmentation, though, including the fragmentation of values, is actually quite typical of urban societies. Unaware of this, disoriented Soviet citizens still ascribe all problems to "Stalinism" or to the evils of the "command-administrative system." However, despite all the talk of chaos, the USSR has not yet seen anything like the British revolt against Prime Minister Thatcher's "poll tax." Some turmoil, as many fear, cannot yet be discarded as a short-term prospect for Russia, but the developing electoral process holds the promise of becoming a means for effecting change without recourse to mass uprisings. The likelihood of widespread civil unrest will decrease as the electoral process enhances the learning ability of the new civic institutions, the emergence of credible leaders, and the nonviolent character of the new social movements.

The second source of distortion arises from Western media coverage, which overdramatizes each novelty. Soon, people inside and outside the USSR will take it for granted that, as in any other country, each month may bring news of protests, strikes, and demonstrations, of organized crime, ethnic violence, anti-Semitism, and other ugly bigotries. By treating such incidents as enormous calamities, the Western media interfere with their audiences' realistic perception of both the real problems facing the USSR and the ongoing activities of healthy forces for change and remediation. For a country that Western reporters often depict as "falling apart," its government so far seems inordinately stable.

———————

Over the past five years we have witnessed a fascinating process that might be called "the education of Gor-

bachev." Nothing in his early career as a party apparat-
chik prepared him for the tasks he undertook as
secretary general, except his knowledge of the apparat,
which proved useful in upending it. But Gorbachev has
had much to learn, and much to unlearn. Once secretary
general of a compromised party, now president of a
much more potent new parliament, Gorbachev has enlarged his vistas, adapted to new realities, and continued to push forward his reform program. Nonetheless,
individuals being what they are—a perishable commodity, after all—the question remains, Will the transformation of the USSR be derailed if Gorbachev disappears
or fails?

For now, my answer oscillates between "probably
not" and "not anymore." The prevailing tendency to discuss the fate of the USSR in terms of Gorbachev's personal chances is characteristic of the media, especially
of the electronic media, which depict complex political
events in terms of the activities of personalities who are
labeled winners and losers. But just as today's fast-
moving events result from processes that unfolded over
decades, their full scope and shape will evolve over the
years to come. The role of the leader, crucial at some
points, may become routine or insignificant at others. It
is conceivable that Gorbachev will one day become a
classroom case study for historiosophical reflection
about the role of personality in history, or about the cult
of "personality" (without the cult of person, though) pro-
mulgated by the media.

Some observers, citing the well-known Russian and
Soviet proneness toward autocracy, are leery of the new
strong presidency. Their caution is justified, but only insofar as there are unsavory potentials in any new institution created in a volatile time; weak governments can
be as dangerous as strong presidencies, and examples

abound of democratically elected parliaments having committed all sorts of nonsense. Quite obviously, the Gorbachev presidency is not strong enough and needs new sources of support. But we can now restate quite firmly that the processes we are witnessing in the USSR are the product of an impersonal historical momentum, one that leaders have to adapt to.

The foundations for a new democratic state system are being laid and will remain no matter who becomes "prezident," as the Russian spelling has it. Elected bodies, political groups and alliances, an active press—all the necessary institutions of a democratic civil society are in place and are doing their homework. Once the transition is completed, the Gorbachev phenomenon will have come to its fruition, and the special role of this individual will have concluded.

In the meantime, some slippage could occur. Quite apart from the problems posed by economic collapse, the weakening of Gorbachev's leadership is built into the political logic of perestroika. Gorbachev was able to launch perestroika because of his mastery of the Soviet government's dual levers of power, those governing the party apparatus and the central ministerial machinery. But perestroika itself implied an end to a statutory one-party system and hence a change in, or even the demise of, the old ruling party. It also implied, as part of the declared democratization process, a redistribution of power between the center, the republics, and the local authorities by means of a credible electoral process. A change in prerogatives and the diminuition of the old central government was thus unavoidable. The latter might even be scrapped altogether in the event that a federation is not reconstituted, or is reconstituted only in very loose form. Whatever the final outcome, however,

Gorbachev's main pillars of support are beginning to wobble. He will be able to remain in power only if some sort of federal body is preserved and again proposes him as candidate for the presidency—and if the general electorate concurs.

Until the transition to democracy is complete, however, the volatility in Soviet affairs continues, and a precipitous unseating of Gorbachev could be extremely damaging to perestroika. It is an almost classic situation for the emergence of demagoguery. If a possible usurper is on the horizon, though, so too are various countervailing trends. But such processes do not obey precise timetables, and costly mishaps may occur. In any event, from the ongoing battle for new political alliances, one will prevail, at least for a period of time, and will continue to renovate the old system according to its political, ideological, and economic vision.

The nature of such an alliance and vision is still an open question. Democracies can produce right-wing, nationalistic majorities and opt for all kinds of strongmen and dictatorial apprentices. Barring this kind of worst-case scenario, it is possible that Gorbachev will face the electorate in 1994 and the voters will decide. (As in most other countries, opinion polls will predict the result before election day.) That such an expectation does not sound outlandish is a measure of the changes that have already occurred in the Soviet system. The education of Gorbachev is now being followed—and will soon be surpassed as a historical reality—by the education of the citizenry, an event quite unprecedented in the history of Russia. From the deepening crisis, a new polity is emerging, one sufficiently capable of coping with the various troubles. All this is very new and momentous, only five years after the still unfinished perestroika was launched.

Decades of neglect and recent failures of judgment or will (sluggishness in offering a new form of commonwealth, hesitations about the economy) are haunting the country and its leaders. For now, even the new and highly promising feats of democratic state-building seem menacing. The republics, including Russia, have elected their own sovereign parliaments and presidents—an instance of democratization that may undermine the government of the USSR and make it redundant. However eerie, this possibility cannot be dismissed, for events are no longer dictated by the leadership. Spontaneity and pressures from below, previously disregarded or misunderstood, are powerful new factors, adding a dimension of unpredictability to the picture. The real and surrealistic coexist, with dramatic and nerve-wracking effects for all concerned.

The specter of dictatorship is also looming large. Political fragmentation and a dangerous crisis of central authority are an almost classic background for such a development.

14

In Search of Clues in the Past

If we want to understand the recent turmoil in the Soviet Union and try to peer into the near future, we need to concentrate much of our attention on the interplay of politics and spontaneity, on political movements and the role of personality, and on the effects of historical trends, especially the massive waves of restructuring brought about by the hectic urbanization of the last thirty to forty years.

The recentness of Soviet urbanization is one of the themes of this book, as is the idea that Soviet urbanization has been complicated by the Soviet style of bureaucratic management. Throughout the postwar period, the old-style bureaucracy seriously hindered the creation and maturing of communal citywide and intracity identities and solidarities, the development of shared cultural, ideological, and moral values. Depoliticization, one of the hallmarks of party rule, only added to the trouble by depriving citizens of the practice of politics.

Events of the 1930s are much discussed these days in

the USSR in search of explanations of "what happened and why it happened"—"it" being Stalinism, of course. This period, in turn, can be best understood by reference to longer-term historical tendencies.

First, one must consider the "extensive" character of much of Russia's historical efforts at solving its problems. Whether state-guided or spontaneous, most Russian efforts have tended to be far-ranging and expansive, but not very deep. A related feature has been the willingness of Russia's autocratic governments to take shortcuts, to distrust slower, more organic development. In a phrase, these governments were unwilling to trust history. Instead, when conditions seemed to demand it—and the West was always a crucial factor here—the Russian regimes would hastily call for large-scale accelerated borrowings of foreign forms and try to impose these on a recalcitrant, archaic, local social structure.

In the version of this historical pattern that occurred in the twentieth century, Russia, and later the USSR, witnessed wave after wave of destruction and forced restructuring, during and after World War I, the civil war, the upheavals of the 1930s, and again during and after World War II. The development of new structures was followed by new or intensified forms of bondage, one step forward in one direction accompanied by one or more steps backward in another—an almost classical repetition of the "Peter the Great syndrome."

In the Soviet period, the authoritarian, but not despotic, policies of Lenin's NEP were replaced by a despotism unique even in a century that gave birth to a number of very vicious despots. The forced acceleration of industrial growth led to a renewed form of agrarian bondage as well as to a specifically industrial helotry.

This coerced industrialization was not followed by a broader modernization; development did not serve the cause of human emancipation. It is in this sense, despite differences in time and ideology, that Stalin's model and Peter's have much in common.

We may now introduce into this historical equation several specific features of the Soviet period that were deeply marked by the preceding period, that is, by the situation that produced the NEP. The historical back-slide wrought by the shattering events after World War I were inherited by the NEP, which was able to restore a peacetime normalcy but would have needed much more time and effort to overcome the combined effects of the archaization wrought by the calamities of 1914–1921 and the reappearing complexities of the new relative re-tardation during the NEP. The shortcut employed from 1929 on was an attempt to weld a modern roof onto a rickety, enfeebled base, in the belief that this operation would do what organic and rather lengthy development had done elsewhere. Political intervention can, of course, accelerate development, but here was a sharp jolt intended to burst the constraints of history. The ef-fort to substitute a monumental shortcut by fiat led to despotism; the power of the whip, it was assumed, would prove much more effective than economic stimulation and more autonomous mass involvement.

An additional noteworthy feature evolved from the massive uprooting of millions of people by collectiviza-tion and the tempos of industrialization under Stalin. The social crisis that resulted from these policies was protracted in character. No less important for our pur-poses is the fact that the widespread social change brought about the promotion of millions of people into new, often more desirable positions. Responsibility and power were bestowed on many who would never have had any such opportunities under the previous system.

The speed of this large-scale social promotion condemned it, at least in the short run, to rely on persons lacking the appropriate cultural and professional preparation for the technical, administrative, and political jobs that the expanding system needed to fill. Most of the new appointees were certainly grateful for the opportunities granted them, but they were insecure in their positions and unsure of their abilities to execute the tasks assigned them. Such crumbly, insecure, unsettled social groups—including those appointed to quite high positions—were an excellent breeding ground for the propagation of all kinds of myths, such as the need for a "strong leader," and scapegoating. In short, they readily accepted, or at least were not immune to, Stalinism.

In sum, coercive development was accompanied by the broad expansion of the tools of despotic fiat. The nondespotic authoritarianism that enabled the whole venture in the first place was supplanted by a system that combined expanding economic activity, cultural and political reaction, and an enormous growth in the bureaucracy—all within the framework of a police state designed to control the population but, no less so, the bureaucracy itself. Again, the same phenomenon: Stalinism.

The tendency to interpret such phenomena by locating their roots in some easily discernible factor is current in Soviet studies. Some propose to fault the Russian intelligentsia for Stalinism, although such a tack does not lead us very far. The 1930s, in particular, were the decade of the *praktiki*—not of the intelligentsia, not even of "the Bolsheviks," both of which groups were either swamped or destroyed and replaced at all rungs by people of rural and worker origins. This observation is not meant to disparage these masses; there was nothing wrong, for example, with the institution of *rabfaki* ("workers' faculties") in the 1920s. But the circumstances and methods of this massive promotion created a climate quite inimical to what we understand by the term *intelligentsia*. This monumental social upsurge, the elevation of poorly "cultured" broad layers into the apparats, could not but offer a fertile soil for cultural mediocrity, to say the least; more correctly, it was a medium for cultural counterrevolution, for Stalinism itself. The cultural vacuum in this disoriented transitional society was also favorable to myths of shaping "a new man," from what could look like the right clay.

Such "shaping" was certainly quite successful for a time, although we do not yet know who actually believed in what during the Stalin era. But we do know that at a later stage, in changed circumstances, "the social matter" changed too, and the "shaping" was no longer effective.

Another example of an interpretational shortcut, one which attempts to explain everything without considering the whole vortex of factors, is still particularly popular. It skips the historical stages, bothers little about predecessors and long-term trends, and educes Minerva straight from Jupiter's head: Stalin came from Lenin, who came from Marx. In this sketch the October Revolution is seen as a whim of Lenin's (with the help of the pathologically radical intelligentsia) or else Lenin's error that he should have spared us. Arguments about Lenin's or Leninism's congenital totalitarianism are another version of the same fallacy. Yet another, broader version states quite simply: The very act of claiming to possess a preferred blueprint for social change and proposing to act on it puts one on a direct road to Stalinism.

Leninism, its roots and heritage, cannot be discussed here in any depth, but we can hint at one problem with this interpretation: Within the history of this movement and ideology a variety of political behaviors are evident, and the movement's leaders, including Lenin, came up with different interpretations and programs for action in response to changing circumstances. Trotsky, Zinoviev, Kamenev, Bukharin, even Stalin—each battled it out against the others and against Lenin, offering different perspectives on such crucial questions as to whether to take power at all—or when, and why not—whether to accept markets, what socialism was or was not, and whether socialism could be built at all in Russia alone. Thus there were alternative possibilities in this movement, and to deduce monolithic uniformity or homogeneity from it is a wholly dubious way of writing history. There were several Leninisms, and it couldn't have been otherwise in the mercurial situation that obtained in revolutionary Russia.

Finally, it is important to emphasize that in order for the sinister potential of Leninism to materialize, the Bolshevik party and most of its Leninist heritage had to be destroyed. The multiple potentials of Bolshevism, as long as it still functioned as a political party or a stream inside the party, were mortally weakened by the social process I outlined earlier; the massive influx of poorly educated adherents of popular extraction favored and fostered the more absolutist trends and potentials of the system. To understand the errors or structural weaknesses in Bolshevism, one must again avoid simplistic formulas. It helps, rather, to realize that Bolshevism as a politico-ideological organization and movement ceased to exist by 1929, although its terms and claims lingered on. The proclivity of ideological constructs to persist long after the demise of the conditions that produced them is well known to historians, and it should not mislead them in this particular case.

One other feature in the fate of Bolshevism can contribute to our understanding of its victory and demise alike. The defeat and destruction of the tsarist ruling strata was brought upon them by their own weaknesses. Tsarist Russia produced classes supposedly ready to compete for political preeminence, but they did not manage to reestablish a political system appropriate to the changing social and economic scene. There was a heavy price to pay for this failure.

The Leninist revolution built a new state organization, but it could not produce a viable social class capable of political power either. The putative ruling class—the proletariat—was in disarray after the civil war, and its members had only low levels of culture. (Of course, one need not accept the Bolshevik idea that a dictatorship of the proletariat was feasible in the first place.) The ruling class that was emerging, surreptitiously—the bureaucracy—was not acceptable at that time and, officially at least, not even later. Out came a substitution arrangement, which Lenin, contrary to all kinds of ideas attributed to him, did not relish at all. So, a party in lieu of a ruling class, a party claiming to be able to represent a broad social interest, was to become the great historical novelty, even if it represented less than it promised.

A leadership network involved with a larger class is not, in itself, exceptional. What counted was the direction events took. The process went, notably in the 1920s, in the direction of depoliticization, the eviction from political participation not only of the citizenry at large but also of party members. The supposedly democratic intention expressed in the admission into the party of hundreds of thousands, even several millions, of politically "innocent" people paradoxically frustrated the party's ability to represent even these members or to evolve a serious ruling elite. Instead, the expansion of membership contributed heavily to deep bureaucratization of the party and to the concentration of power in a very narrow apex. The hectic changes created by the big drive of the 1930s reproduced the same problems and dilemmas on an even larger scale. Not only was the party swamped by newcomers several times over, but bureaucratization now became all-embracing, and the problem of creating a serious, broad ruling class, or a willing alliance of social forces ready and capable of producing one, could not be resolved.

Stalinist despotism was a result and an expression of precisely this situation. The state system did not have a large enough ruling class and actually prevented one from emerging. By then, the working class had lost even the aspiration, let alone the possibility, of acceding to real power. And the bureaucracy, or its top layers, which now became the obvious contender for this role, was prevented from achieving it by Stalin's purges. Obviously, Stalin was willing to do anything in order not to find himself presiding over a constituted ruling class that would certainly want to impose its will on him. In any case, this bureaucracy was still socially crumbly, and Stalin was successful in deliberately perpetuating this crumbliness.

After Stalin's death the upper layers of Soviet officialdom did produce an effective ruling class. The overwhelming majority of officials wielding any degree of power were in the party—by then an enormous organization, 18 million strong—and the party became the mouthpiece for the top bureaucracy. At that, in essence, the party ceded power to the ministerial bureaucracy, which was running the show and reaping the benefits almost at will. There was nothing—so it seemed to the bureaucrats—that the party could do to them, except demote a minister or a deputy.

Overall rather peaceful and gradual, the post-Stalin period was dominated by a powerful urbanization. This was essentially a spontaneous process, with little state coercion involved. But because the entire social structure was again reshaped, in such a short span of time, this spontaneous urbanization was in many ways no less traumatic than earlier coercive drives. Moreover, this time conditions were ripening for the bureaucratic system itself to lose its potency. The system's congenital sclerosis spread and clogged it beyond repair.

From 1950 on, the USSR was hard hit by both the general, typical effects of urbanization and by the particular effects stemming from the speed and relative newness of the process in Soviet culture. The emergence of a ruling bureaucratic class was itself one of these effects; the causes of its fall a few decades later came from the same caldron. After Stalin's death, as the ruling networks settled into their monopolistic position, a new pretendent for sharing or even usurping power emerged from the social process: the broad term for it, which we have used earlier, is *civil society*. Neither Khrushchev nor Kosygin, however, responded to this new sociopolitical reality. It is at this juncture that Gorbachev's perestroika, and the character of the crisis it faces, must be located.

As the study of history shows, the Soviets have experimented with three different models or patterns of the state-cum-economy relationship. One is the "plan-and-market" model tried during the NEP. The second is the full-fledged bureau-administrative pattern as it developed after Stalin's death. During the intervening Stalinist period, the former model was discarded and the ground was prepared for the latter. All three models were feasible—each was put into practice—and all three turned out to be relatively short-lived. Except that the shortest, the NEP, seems to be coming to life again, in new circumstances, allowing this time also for an entirely new dimension that the two others repressed—namely, political democracy.

The exhaustion of the post-Stalinist bureau-administrative system and the causes of its demise are related to the stormy and shattered social scene of the 1930s and its peculiar policies of "administered" development. The sum total of the methods produced a system that looked extremely powerful, but contained within itself the mechanism of its self-destruction. The state erected an economy without economics, an economy oblivious to costs; a planning system without a real plan, a methodlessness that produced damaging imbalances; and a political system without politics and utterly inattentive to the growing civil society. These parallels are not accidental: the economic and political functions were intertwined, and politically warranted by the party.

Neither the political environment nor the state system were conducive to the judicious handling of the unsettled, still crumbly social landscape. The poor state of integration within urban Soviet society, the novelty—poorly understood by both citizens and scholars—of a broad urban society, made for a bewildered people. Nor were the politically and intellectually bankrupt power-holders able to respond to this new reality. And so, the system was guaranteed a dubious "success": it was allowed, with impunity, to work out to the full its self-destructive features, until they brought the country to a dead end. And to perestroika, with its continuing uncertainties and surprises, including the much talked about right wing takeover in the name of law and order.

Such a takeover, though a realistic prospect, has little chance to deal with the basic problems of the country and may easily turn out to be even more fragile than the fledgling democracy the right would like to displace.

So the wheel is turning and will continue to turn for some time to come, until a more settled system emerges, probably in the near future. It is still an open-ended question what shape this new system will take.

Bibliography

This bibliography is highly selective, containing only the books and articles that I consulted on specific topics in writing this book.

1. Afanas'ev, V. G. *Chelovek v upravlenii obshchestvom*. Moscow, 1977.

2. Anchishkin, A. "Novoe kachestvo ekonomicheskogo rosta." *Voprosy Ekonomiki* 9 (1986).

3. Anikst, A. M. *Kul'turnoe stroitel'stvo v piatiletke*. Moscow and Leningrad, 1930.

4. Anokhina, L. A., and M. N. Shmeleva. *Byt gorodskogo naseleniia srednei polosy RSFSR v proshlom i nastoiashchem*. Moscow, 1977.

5. Antonov, S. "Kar'iera–zapiski slesaria-instrumental'-shchika." *Nash Sovremennik*, nos. 1–3, 1975.

6. Arutiunian, Iu. V. *Sotsial'naia struktura sel'skogo naseleniia SSSR*. Moscow, 1971.

7. Baranov, A. V. *Sotsial'no-demograficheskoe razvitie krupnogo goroda*. Moscow, 1981.

8. Bonk, E. L. "Ob odnoi probleme sotsiologicheskikh issledovanii obshchestvennogo mneniia o prave." *Sovetskoe Gosudarstvo i Pravo* 8 (1986).

9. Borshchevskii, V. G., S.V. Uspenskii, and O. I. Shkaratan. *Gorod: Metodologicheskie problemy kompleksnogo sotsial'nogo i ekonomicheskogo planirovaniia.* Moscow, 1975.

10. Braudel, Fernand. *Afterthoughts on Material Civilization and Capitalism.* Baltimore, 1977.

11. Braudel, Fernand. *Identité de la France: Espace et histoire.* Paris, 1986.

12. *Chislennost' i sostav naseleniia SSSR po dannym Vsesoiuznoi perepisi naseleniia 1979 goda.* Moscow, 1984.

13. Cohen, Stephen R. *Rethinking the Soviet Experience: Politics and History Since 1917.* New York, 1986.

14. Danilov, V. P. *Sovetskaia dokolkhoznaia derevnia—naselenie, chislennost', khoziaistvo.* Moscow, 1977.

15. Demidenko, E. S. *Demograficheskie problemy bol'shikh gorodov.* Moscow, 1980.

16. Dobrynin, A. "Glavnaia sotsial'naia sila sovremennosti." *Kommunist* 16 (1986).

17. Dodge, Norton T. *Women in the Soviet Economy.* Baltimore, 1966.

18. *XXVII s'ezd Kommunisticheskoi Partii Sovetskogo Soiuza, 25 fevralia–6 marta 1986 goda, Stenograficheskii otchet.* 2 vols. Moscow, 1986.

19. Duby, George, ed. *L'Histoire de la France urbaine.* Vol. 4. Paris, 1983.

20. *Ezhegodnik 1984 Sovetskoi Assotsiatsii politicheskikh nauk.* Moscow, 1985.

21. Fitzpatrick, Sheila. *Education and Social Mobility in the Soviet Union, 1921–1934.* New York, 1979.

22. Gordon, L. A., and E. V. Klopov. "Razvitie sotsial'noi struktury sovetskogo goroda." *Rabochii Klass i Sovremennyi Mir* 6 (1973).

23. Gordon, L. A., and V. V. Komarovskii. "Dinamika sotsi-al'no-professional'nogo sostava pokolenii." *Sotsiologicheskie Issledovaniia* 3 (1986).

24. Goriunov, S. P., and F. M. Lew. "Obshchestvennoe mnenie o proizvodstvennoi situatsii," *Sotsiologicheskie Issledovaniia* 2 (1986).

25. Gregory, Paul R., and Robert C. Stuart. *Comparative Economic Systems.* Boston, 1980.

26. Gregory, Paul R., and Robert C. Stuart. *Soviet Economic Structure and Performance.* 3d ed. New York, 1986.

27. Habermas, Jürgen. *Critical Debates.* Cambridge, Mass., 1982.

28. Hamm, Michael F. *The City in Russian History.* Lexington, Kent., 1976.

29. Harris, Chauncy D. *Cities of the Soviet Union.* Chicago, 1970.

30. Hough, Jerry, and Merle Fainsod. *How the Soviet Union Is Governed.* Cambridge, Mass., 1979.

31. Iagodin, G. "Vysshee obrazovanie: sostoianie i perspektivy perestroiki." *Kommunist* 16 (1986).

32. Ianitskii, O. N. *Urbanizatsiia, nauchno-tekhnichheskaia revoliutsiia i rabochii klass.* Moscow, 1972.

33. Ianitskii, O. N. *Urbanizatsiia, gorod, chelovek: kritika burzhuaznoi sotsiologii.* Moscow, 1974.

34. Ianitskii, O. N. "Chelovecheskii faktor sotsialisticheskoi urbanizatsii: stanovlenie novykh orientirov." *Sotsiologicheskie Issledovaniia* 2 (1986).

35. *Itogi vsesoiuznoi perepisi naseleniia SSSR, 1959 g., svodnyi tom.* Moscow, 1962.

36. Iudin, I. M. *Sotsial'naia baza rosta KPSS.* Moscow, 1973.

37. Ivanov, V. N. "Sotsiologicheskoe obespechenie intensifikatsii ekonomiki." *Sotsiologicheskie Issledovaniia* 2 (1986).

38. Kainz, Howard. *Hegel's Philosophy of Right, with Marx's Comments*. The Hague, 1974.

39. Katsura, A. V. Article in *Sistemnye Issledovaniia: metodologicheskie problemy. Ezhegodnik 1985*, edited by D. N. Gvishiani. Moscow, 1986.

40. Kaufmann, Walter. *Hegel, an Interpretation*. New York, 1967.

41. Kerblay, Basile. *L'Isba Russe d'hier et d'aujourd'hui*. Lausanne, 1973.

42. Kerblay, Basile. *Modern Soviet Society*. Translated by Rubert Swyer. New York, 1983.

43. Kerblay, Basile, and Marie Lavigne. *Les Soviétiques des années 80*. Paris, 1985.

44. Kershaw, Ian. *The Nazi Dictatorship: Problems and Perspectives of Interpretation*. London, 1985.

45. Kharchev, A. G. "Issledovaniia sem'i: na poroge novogo etapa." *Sotsiologicheskie Issledovaniia* 2 (1986).

46. Khorev, B. S. *Gorodskie poseleniia SSSR (problemy rosta i ikh izucheniia)*. Moscow, 1968.

47. Khorev, B. S., ed. *Malyi gorod: sotsial'no-demograficheskoe issledovanie nebol'shogo goroda*. Moscow, 1972.

48. Khorev, B. S., and B. M. Kiseleva. *Urbanizatsiia i demograficheskie protsessy*. Moscow, 1982.

49. Kim, M. P., ed. *Velikaia Oktiabr'skaia sotsialisticheskaia revoliutsiia i stanovlenie sovetskoi kul'tury, 1917–1927*. Moscow, 1985.

50. Kolganov, A. "Protivorechiia tsentralizma i samodeiatel'nosti." *Voprosy Ekonomiki* 9 (1986).

51. Kornai, Jànos. *Growth, Shortage and Efficiency: A Microdynamic Model of the Socialist Economy*. Berkeley and Los Angeles, 1982.

52. Kozyrin, Vladimir. "Prochnaia svarka—zapiski zavodskogo mastera." *Nash Sovremennik* 8 (1972).

53. *Krupneishie goroda—ikh nastoiashchee i budushchee*. Moscow, 1979.

54. Kupriianov, L. V. *Goroda Severnogo Kavkaza vo vtoroi polovine XIX veka*. Moscow, 1981.
55. Kurman, M.V., and I. V. Lebedinskii. *Naselenie bol'shogo sotsialisticheskogo goroda*. Moscow, 1968.
56. Kvasha, A. Ia. *Problemy ekonomiko-demograficheskogo razvitiia SSSR*. Moscow, 1974.
57. Labuteva, T. "Zaniatiia naseleniia SSSR." *Vestnik Statistiki* 6 (1974).
58. Lane, David. *The Socialist Industrial State*. London, 1976.
59. Lenin, V. I. *KPSS, O rabote partiinogo i gosudarstvennogo apparata*. Moscow, 1976.
60. Lenin, V. I. *Polnoe Sobranie sochinenii*. 5th ed. Vol. 45. Moscow, 1964.
61. Lewin, Moshe. *Political Undercurrents in Soviet Economic Debates*. Princeton, N. J., 1984.
62. Lewin, Moshe. *The Making of the Soviet System*. New York, 1985.
63. Lewis, Robert A., and Richard F. Roland. "Urbanization in Russia and the USSR: 1917–1970." In *The City in Russian History*, edited by Michael F. Hamm. Lexington, Kent., 1976.
64. Ligachev, E. K., and others. In *Kommunist* 15 (1986).
65. Lorimer, F. *The Population of the Soviet Union: History and Prospects*. Geneva, 1946.
66. Marx, K., and F. Engels. *Sochineniia*. 2d ed. Vol. 1. Moscow, 1955.
67. Morton, Henry W., and Robert C. Stuart, eds. *The Contemporary Soviet City*. New York, 1984.
68. Moskovskii, A. S., and V. A. Isupov. *Formirovanie gorodskogo naseleniia Sibiri (1926–1939)*. Novosibirsk, 1984.
69. *Narodnoe khoziaistvo SSSR 1980*. Moscow, 1980.
70. *Narodnoe khoziaistvo SSSR 1983*. Moscow, 1984.
71. *Narodnoe khoziaistvo SSSR, 1922–1982*. Moscow, 1982.
72. *Naselenie, trudovye resursy SSSR—problemy razmeshcheniia i puti ikh resheniia*. Moscow, 1971.

73. Nemchinov, V. S. Article in *Izbrannye Proizvedeniia* 4 (1967).

74. *New Statesman*, review by Sheila Rowbotham, January 30, 1987.

75. *New York Times*, editorial, November 24, 1986.

76. *New York Times*, January 17, 1987. Dispatch, "Atomic Agency Cites Chernobyl Safety Rules."

77. Parygin, B. D., ed. *Nauchno-tekhnicheskaia revoliutsiia i sotsial'naia psikhologiia; materialy mezhgorodskoi konferentsii*. Moscow, 1981.

78. Parygin, B. D., ed. *Sotsial'no-psikhologicheskie problemy nauchno-tekhnologicheskogo progressa*. Moscow, 1982.

79. Perez-Diaz, Victor M. *State, Bureaucracy and Civil Society*. London, 1978.

80. Pisarev, I. Iu. *Naselenie i trud v SSSR*. Moscow, 1966.

81. Rabinovich, M. G. *Ocherki etnografii russkogo feodal'nogo goroda—gorozhane, ikh obshchestvennyi i domashnii byt*. Moscow, 1978.

82. *Rabochi Klass i Sovremennyi Mir* 6 (1973).

83. Rashin, A. G. "Rost gorodskogo naseleniia SSSR." *Istoricheskie Zapiski* 66 (1985).

84. Rogovin, V. Z. "Sotsial'naia spravedlivost' i sotsialisticheskoe raspredelenie." *Voprosy Filosofii* 9 (1986).

85. Rutkevich, M. N. "Sotsialisticheskaia spravedlivost'." *Sotsiologicheskie Issledovaniia* 3 (1986).

86. Safarov, R. A. *Obshchestvennoe mnenie i gosudarstvennoe upravlenie*. Moscow, 1975.

87. Sbytov, V. F. "Shtrikhi k portretu sovetskoi nauchno-tekhnicheskoi intelligentsii." *Sotsiologicheskie Issledovaniia* 3 (1986).

88. Selunskaia, V. M., ed. *Izmeneniia sotsial'noi struktury narodov SSSR*. Moscow, 1981.

89. Seniavskii, S. L. *Izmeneniia v sotsial'noi strukture sovetskogo obshchestva, 1938–1970*. Moscow, 1973.

90. Seniavskii, S. L. Article in *Sotsial'no-ekonomicheskie problemy razvitogo sotsializma v SSSR*. Moscow, 1976.

91. Shkaratan, O. I. *Problemy sotsial'noi struktury rabochego klassa*. Moscow, 1970.

92. Shkaratan, O. I., ed. *Etno-sotsial'nye problemy goroda*. Moscow, 1986.

93. Shumakov, S. L. "Proizvodstvennaia tema v kinomatografe." *Sotsiologicheskie Issledovaniia* 3 (1986).

94. Snesarev, G. A., ed. *Izmeneniia sotsial'noi struktury sovetskogo obshchestva*. Moscow, 1976.

95. *Sotsial'noe razvitie rabochego klassa SSSR; istoriko-sotsiologicheskii ocherk*. Moscow, 1971.

96. Southall, Aidan, ed. *Urban Anthropology: Crosscultural Studies of Urbanization*. New York, 1973.

97. *Sovetskaia Istoricheskaia Entsiklopediia*. Vol. 8. Moscow, 1985.

98. Spirin, L. M. *Klassy i partii v grazhdanskoi voine v Rossii (1917–1920)*. Moscow, 1968.

99. *SSSR v tsifrakh v 1984 godu*. Moscow, 1985.

100. *Statisticheskii spravochnik SSSR za 1928 g*. Moscow, 1929.

101. *Statisticheskoe Obozrenie* 5 (1928).

102. Strumilin, S. G. "Dinamika krest'ianskogo khoziaistva za 1917–1922 gody." In *Krest'ianshoe khoziaistvo za vremiia revoliutsii*, edited by P. Pershin. Moscow, 1923.

103. *Tiazhest' oblozheniia v SSSR*. Moscow, 1929.

104. Trotsky, Leon. "Towards Capitalism or Socialism." In *The Challenge of the Left Opposition*, edited by Naomi Allen. New York, 1975.

105. Urlanis, V. Ts. *Zhizn' pokoleniia*. Moscow, 1968.

106. Vas'kina, L. I. "K izucheniiu chislennosti gorodov i gorodskogo naseleniia SSSR." In *Russkii gorod*, (*istoriko-metodologicheskii sbornik*), edited by V. M. Ianin. Moscow, 1976.

107. Vas'kina, L. I. *Rabochii Klass SSSR nakanune sotsialisti-cheskoi industriializatsii (chislennost', sostav, razme-shchenie)*. Moscow, 1981.

108. Walker, Martin. *The Waking Giant: Gorbachev's Russia*. New York, 1986.

109. Weber, Max. *The City*. New York and London, 1958.

110. Zaslavskaia, T. "Perestroika i sotsiologiia." *Pravda*, February 6, 1987.

Index

Academic freedom, 66, 69; and the advantages of the "invisible college," 73

Academy of Sciences, 76, 86; Association of Political Sciences, 89; Research Institute in Social Interdisciplinary Studies, 92; Soviet Sociological Association of, 88–89; and systems analysis, 90

Adaptation to urban life, 69–70. *See also* Ruralization of cities

Agrarian economic development, 13–20; by entrepreneurial classes, 13; and the shift from agriculture to industry, 53; socioeconomic context of, 14–20; under Stalinism, 21–22; state policies on, 13–14, 21; in tsarist Russia, 13–17

Agrarian nexus, 15, 20; and Stalinism, 21–22, 24

Alcohol abuse, 76, 110; anti-alcohol campaign, 162; Gorbachev's policies on, 116; laws on, 77

Andropov, Yuri V., 114

Artistic productions, public opinion influenced by, 75

Arutiunian, Iu. V., 16

"Atomized society," 5, 6

Authoritarian coercion, 152

Authoritarian management styles, 94

Autocracy, 171

Autonomy of the individual, 64–67. *See also* Individuals

Benjamin, Walter, 44

Beria, Laurenty Pavlovich, 101

Birthrates, decline of, 68

Black market, 141

Bolshevik party, democratic procedures of, 134–35; destruction of, 180

Bolsheviks, 59, 178–179

Bolshevism, 180–181

Bonk, E. L., 76–77

"Bourgeois" experts and specialists, 58, 59. *See also* Specialists

"Branch principle," 109

Bratsk, Siberia, 106

Braudel, Fernand, 19, 36; socioeconomic theory of, 17–18

Brezhnev, Leonid I., 2, 114
Brzezinski, Zbigniew, 103
Bukharin, Nikolai, 180; on the state bureaucracy, 109
Bureaucracy: demoralization and corruption of, 103–4; development of, 22–23, 178, 181; effects of the state-economy-party triad on, 112–13; "interest groups" in, 103, 105; linked with economic and political malfunctions, 104–7; and opposition to Gorbachev's policies, 127, 167; party apparatus merged with, 109–10; planning and management systems of, 104–11; power of, 109, 112–13; reforms in, by Khrushchev, 60, 102; self-defense and self-preservation techniques of, 26, 109; and state-cum-economy relationship, 184. *See also* Ministerial bureaucracy
"Bureaucratic utopia," myth of, 151

Cadres: and bureaucratic growth, 22–23; education of, 59; effect of Stalinist purges on, 59; intellectuals as, 50; modernization of, 61–62; and social justice, 118
Capitalism: and agrarian reform, 14–15, 18; derived from rural vs. urban markets, 19; in the socioeconomic theory of F. Braudel, 17–18
Censorship, reduction of, 116
Central Research Sector on Social Psychology, 88
Chernenko, Konstantin U., 114

Chernobyl nuclear accident, 113–14
Chiesa, Julietto, 167
Churches, 7
Cities, 30–42; building of, 104, 106, 108; definition of, 39–40; and integrated urban-rural development, 41. *See also* Urbanization
Citizenry and state relations, 131
"Civic courage" to discuss national problems, 115
Civil society, 146, 160, 172, 183, 184; defined, 80; and Soviet political history, viii, 81–82; under statism, 80–81, 157, 158
Civil unrest, 170
Civil war, 24–25, 176, 181; effect of, on agrarian reform, 15, 16, 17, 18; effect of, on the professional classes, 58; and historical stages, 151; and models of Soviet history, 152
Coercive development, 178
Cohen, Stephen F., 2
Cold wars, 3
Collaboration between social scientists and politicians, 86–87, 95
"Collective" political leadership, 60, 102
Collectivization, peasant response to, 26
COMECON. *See* Council for Mutual Economic Assistance
"Command-administrative system," 170
Communal agriculture, 15–16; and the peasant response to collectivization, 26
Communes, construction of, 106

Communications: growth of, 46, 57; public opinion influenced by, 70–71, 72

Concentration camps, 21, 27; decline of, 60, 102

Constitution, 161

"Constitutionalism," 102

Construction industry: growth of, 46; and ministerial planning, 104, 106, 108

Consumer goods, quality of, 139–40. *See also* Warehouses

Contact groups, 74. *See also* Groups; Informal structures

Costs and expenditures vs. income and profits, 107

Council for Mutual Economic Assistance (COMECON), 168

Criminal deviance, 110

Cultural revolution, and the emancipation of women, 48

Culture: autonomy of, ix; control of, 113; diversity in, xi, 5; and government crisis of legitimacy, 113; interconnection with economy, society, and politics, ix, 4–5, 61–62, 64, 69–70, 110, 113, 117, 122, 123, 130, 146; official "thaws" in, 1–2, 119; and public opinion, 78–79; reforms of, 116; relationship of, with Stalinism, 26–27, 59

Democracy, 158, 184

Democratization, 172, 173, 174; elite support of, 148–49; future of, 132–34; by the Gorbachev administration, 117, 120, 126, 127, 131–32, 134–35; in a one-party political system, 133–34, 150–51; of the party,

131–32; and the Soviet crisis, 158; of the workplace, 131

Demography, 85; and decline of urban birthrates, 68; and the growth of Soviet urban society, 30–32, 145–46; and urban family life, 68

Demoralization, 104, 110. *See also* "Motivational crisis"

"Departmental blurs," 106

"Departmentalism": defined, 104; linked with economic and political malfunctions, 104–7

Depoliticization, 181–82

Despotism, 176, 177, 178; origins of, 23; and peasant communes, 16–17

Destalinization, 1–2

Determinism, 100

Dobrynin, Anatoly, 120, 127

Drug abuse, 110

Drunkenness, 76. *See also* Alcohol abuse

Ecology: and bureaucratic planning, 106–7; public opinion on, 79

"Economic mechanism," 136

Economic organizations, relationship with the state, 141

Economic reform: and consumer power, 140; difficulties of, 164–65; and the education of the labor force, 143; and the future of small business, 141; genesis of, 138–39; Gorbachev's policies on, 116–17, 123, 136–37; and the market economy, 138–39, 140–42; new-line policies on, 137–44; in the 1960s, viii, 1; potential of, 137–38; and the quality of

Economic reform (*continued*)
consumer goods, 139–40; relationship with political reform, viii–ix, 137; scholarly approach to, 137; skeptical attitudes toward, viii, 1–2; and worker autonomy and participation, 142

Economy: as emergency system, 164; failure of, 157; government efforts for the improvement of, 107, 109; and individual rights, 66; and job dissatisfaction, 56, 92, 110; linked with culture, society, and politics, viii–ix, 4–5, 7, 8, 61–62, 64, 69–70, 110, 113, 117, 122, 123, 130, 146; malfunctions and ministerial planning of, 104–7, 174; managed by the state-economy-party triad, 112–13; mathematical science applied to, 2; multisectoral, 164; and the production of unsalable goods, 107, 108, 136; role of the working class in, 46, 142; strategies for the improvement of, 107–10; waste and shortages in, 107–8

Economy, management and planning of: economic malfunctions generated by, 104–7, 184; future of, 142; Gorbachev's new-line policies on, 114–15; and the potential for economic reform, 136–38; by the state-economy-party triad, 112–13

Education: of citizenry, 173; of engineers, 92; Khrushchev's reform plans for, 74; of the labor force, 47–48, 52, 143; of the peasantry, 47; of political cadres, 59; and the power of public opinion, 74; by press, 160; qualitative growth of, 46, 49, 52; quantitative growth of, 47–48; reforms of, 74, 116; on sexual and marital behavior, 68; and social change, 147; in social sciences and ideological disciplines, 115; of Soviet sociologists, 86; of specialists, 46–47, 49, 52; standards for, 47, 48; of technicians, 50; of women, 47–48

Electoral process, 170

Electorate, 173

Elite, 58; attitudes toward democratization, 148–49; effect of Stalinist purges on, 59–60; emergence of, 147; responsibilities of, 148. *See also* Professionals

Eltsin, Boris, 118, 119, 163–164

"Employee participation," 142

"Employees," defined, 46. *See also* Intelligentsia; Specialists

Engineers, education and job dissatisfaction of, 92

Ethnicity, 95–96

Ethnography, 85

Europe: Central, 167; Eastern, 159, 167; Western, 168

European Community, 168

Extramarital pregnancies, 68

Factories: bureaucratic planning linked with economic malfunctions of, 105–6, 107; education of workers in, 143; managers of, 138

Family: individual autonomy catalyzed by, 66–67; urban problems of, 68

Federation, 172–73
Five-year plans, x, 4
Foreign investors, 141
Frankness by political leaders, 114–16, 126
Freedom: of communications and information, 96; of criticism, 119; of movement, 64, 96, 106; of scholars, 65–66, 69, 73
Free markets, 140. *See also* Market economy

Galbraith, John Kenneth, 100
General secretaries, 159, 160; change of, 9
Generational approach to social change, 52–55, 146
Germany, 168–69
Glasnost, x–xi, 160, 169–170; practices of, 116, 118, 119, 131
Gorbachev, Mikhail S., 112–28, 164, 166, 168, 172–73; democratization policies of, 117, 120, 126, 127, 131–32, 134–35, 159, 163, 168; education of, 170–71, 173; future of, 121, 124, 126, 129, 132, 133, 148–49, 150; as general secretary, 1, 114, 171; political support of by intellectuals and professionals, 124, 131–32; new-line policies of, 114–21 (*see also* New line of the Gorbachev administration); opposition to, 120, 126–27, 128, 129; and the party, 114–15, 116, 117, 118, 125–26, 127–28, 130–33, 171; policies of, on "intensification" and quality improvement, 110–11, 139–40, 143; political inheritance of, 112, 114; as president, 172; on

public opinion and public debate, 78, 116; reform policies of, ix–x, 116–20, 123, 126, 160, 163; and renovation of the political process, 124–26, 127–28, 130–32, 134; response of, to social change, 117, 122, 123; revolution conceptualized by, 124; and the rise of the social sciences, 85, 97; and thaws in the arts and culture, 119; vision of, ix–x, 120; working class political support of, 124. *See also* New line of the Gorbachev administration
Gorbachev phenomenon, x, 150, 158, 159, 172
Gordon, L. A., 52–55, 167
Government, 170
Grain supply, 21
Griffiths, Franklyn, 103
Groups: and individual autonomy fostered by urban family life, 66–67; interpretation of mass communications by, 70–71, 72, 75

Habermas, Jürgen, 110
Harris, Chauncy, 30–31, 45
Historical stages: change from "extensive" to "intensive" stages, 100; compression of, 146; concept of, vii–viii; modern, ix; and the revolutionary war, 151; and urbanization, 38
History: and the current crisis, 158; interconnection between politics, society, and culture in, 4–5, 6–8; "laws" of, 100; of the "present," vii (*see also* Historical stages); role of the state in, 4–5, 28

Hitler, Adolf, 3, 8
Hough, Jerry, 103
Housing in tsarist Russia, 20
Human capital, concept of, 98
"Human factor" in Soviet social sciences, 97, 99
Human relations: and the emergence of informal structures, 74; increased emphasis on, 64; and personal communications, 70–71, 72; and urban adaptation fostered by small groups, 69–70. *See also* Individuals
Huntington, Samuel P., 103
Hypothesis of induced reaction, 91

Ianitskii, O. N., 65
Iashin, Aleksandr, 150
Ideological change, 2, 169; and group interpretation of the mass media, 70–71; resistance to, 27
Ideology: and a crisis of legitimacy, 113; and economic reform, 165; "end of," 169; Gorbachev's new-line policies on, 115; public attitudes toward, 115; teaching of, 115
Individuals: and academic freedom, 66; autonomy of, linked with urbanization and urban family life, 63–64, 66–68; freedom of, connected with the scientific-technological revolution, 65–66; and group response to mass media and propaganda, 70–71; moral and psychic health of, 63–64; and morale in the workplace, 93–94; political response to the autonomy of, 68–71;

rights of, 64, 66; and social reforms by the Gorbachev administration, 117
Industrialization, viii, 176–77; and agrarian economic development, 15, 53; and the emergence of a new labor force, 44–47, 53; historical stage of, 38, 44. *See also* Urbanization
Informal structures, 73–75; defined, 73; public opinion influenced by, 75. *See also* Groups
Information: access to, 116, 117, 130; processing of, 54, 55
Institutions, 7–8
Intellectuals. *See* Intelligentsia
Intellectual urban workforce, rise of, 44–45, 54
Intelligentsia, viii, 57–62, 164, 178–79; and educational standards, 47–48; equated with specialists, 46–47; Gorbachev's policies supported by, 124, 143; as government executives, 50; history of, 48–49, 57–60; and meaningful participation in the political system, 123; and the modernization of top cadres, 61–62; new-line economic reforms supported by, 143; party participation by, 131–32; perestroika opposed by, 167; rights demanded by, 64; and Stalinism, 178
"Intensification," 110, 143
Interdisciplinary collaboration between politicians and social scientists, 95, 97–98
Interest groups in the Soviet bureaucracy, 103
Intergenerational social change, 54, 61

International Atomic Energy Agency, 114
Interpretational shortcuts, 178–79
Intragenerational changes in the labor force, 52–55
"Invisible college" of scholars, 66, 69; advantages of, 73
Ivanov, V. N., 92–93

Job dissatisfaction, 92; causes of, 56, 110. *See also* Labor force

Kamenev, Lev Borisovich, 180
Katsura, A. V., 91
Kazakh wilderness, 41
Kazennoe, 115–16
K.G.B., 114
Kharchev, A. G., on urban family life, 68
Khrushchev, Nikita, 183; and bureaucratic demoralization, 103–4; bureaucratic reforms by, 60, 102; on educational reform, 74; party political institutions and party power restored by, 101–2; and the power of political opinion, 74; reforms by, viii, 1–2, 60, 74, 101–2, 129
Klopov, E. V., 167
Kolkhoz peasants, 28; compared with the urban working class, 46; education of, 47; frankness and political freedom of, 150; response to collectivization, 25–26; and the structure of the labor force, 51. *See also* Peasants
Komarovskii, V. V., on generational change in the labor force, 52–55

Kompleksnyi and economic planning, 108
Komsomol league, 69, 78
Kornai, Jànos, on the Soviet economy, 107–8
Kosygin, Aleksei, 183; reforms by, viii, 1–2, 62

Labor force, 43–56; changes in, correlated with political change, 61; components of, 51–52; education of, 47–48, 52; "employees" in, 46; for intellectual work, 44–45, 46–49, 50; intragenerational changes in, 52–55; morale of, 93–94, 107, 110; for physical work, 44–45, 51, 53; and the replacement of the peasantry by an urban working class, 45–46, 53–54; response of, to problems caused by bureaucratic planning, 106; restructuring of, 51–56, 61; self-defense tactics of, 25; "specialists" in, 46–47, 48, 49, 50, 51, 52 (*see also* Specialists); structural imbalance in, 50–51; women in, 48
Landowners, 14; effect of the revolutionary war on, 15
Law: on drunkenness and alcoholism, 77; and the power of public opinion, 76–77; reforms by Nikita Khrushchev, 102; in systems analysis, 91
Legislation, 164
Lenin, Nikolai, 179, 180; on capitalism and the peasant market economy, 19; New Economic Policy (NEP) of, 15, 20, 24, 52, 59, 152, 176, 177;

Lenin, Nikolai (*continued*)
  on the Russian peasantry, 17;
  and totalitarianism, 179
Leningrad University, 76
Leninism, 179, 180
Leninist revolution, 181
"Levers" (A. Iashin), 150
Liberalism, 99
Libraries, 20
Lichnost, 63
Ligachev, Egor, 117
Literature, 160

"Manufacturing villages," 106
Market economy, 17, 169, 180;
  and economic reform, 138–39,
  140–42, 165; in rural vs. urban environments, 19
Marriage, and urban family
  problems, 68
Marx, Karl, 179; on capitalism,
  19; on peasant "mirs," 16
Marxism-Leninism, 2
Mass media, 71, 171. *See also*
  Media
Mathematical models in social
  sciences, 87
Media, 71; and distortion of social changes, 170; and "end of
  ideology," 169; group vs. individual interpretation of, 70–
  71, 75; role of press, 160; and
  public opinion in periodicals,
  75–76; and role of leader, 171
Megacities, 41. *See also* Cities;
  Urbanization
Microworlds, 63–71; of the family, 66–68; of the individual,
  63–66; mass media interpreted by, 70–71; and the
  "motivational crisis," 110; political response to, 68–71, 110;
  of scholars, 66, 69; and state

neglect of social change, 110;
  and urban adaptation by migrant workers, 69
Migration: and adaptation to
  urban life, 35, 69; by rural
  peasants, 20, 22, 28, 34–38; by
  textile workers, 69
Military, and the quality of consumer products, 139–40
Miliukov, Paul, 5
Ministerial bureaucracy, 104–
  11, 182–83; and economic reform, 107–11, 139
Mirs, 37; and despotism, 16–17
Modernization, 177; of cadres,
  51–62; and the socializing
  role of the family, 67
Monomakh, Vladimir, 28
Morale of the labor force, 93–
  94, 107, 110
"Moral vacuum," 167
Moscow: central bureaucratic
  agencies in, 104, 105; University of, 76
Moscow Diary (W. Benjamin),
  44
"Motivational crisis," 104;
  causes of, 106–7, 110

National elections, 131
National interest vs. the bureaucracy, 105
Nationalism, 163, 165–66, 167,
  173
National problems, public debate on, 116, 118
Nazi Germany, 3
New Course, The (L. Trotsky),
  109
New Economic Policy (NEP),
  15, 52, 59, 152, 176, 177; and
  agrarian economic reform, 20;
  linked with social change, 24;

and "plan and market"
model, 184
New line of the Gorbachev
administration, 114–21; on
democratization, 117, 120,
126, 127, 131–35; on economic
management and planning,
114–15, 136–42; on economic
reform, 137–44; on frankness,
114; future of, 121, 129, 148–
49, 150; on ideology, 115; opposition to, 120, 126–27, 128,
129; on party corruption, 119;
and party legitimacy, 125–26;
on public debate on national
problems, 116; on public
opinion, 117; public support
of, 120; on reforms, 116–20;
"rethinking" approach to,
120–21; on revitalization of
the political system, 123, 124–
26, 127–28, 130–32, 134; on
social justice among political
leaders, 118–19
1920s, 179, 181
1930s, 175–76, 178, 184

Obedience, 27
Obshchestvennost, 75
October revolution, 179
Officials, 46; and the structure
of the labor force, 51
Okudzava, Bulat, 78
One-party system, 135, 159, 172;
democratization of, 133–34,
150–51
Opposition to Gorbachev's poli-
cies, 120, 126–27, 128, 129

Parliament, 161, 171–72
Party, 161, 164, 171, 181–82;
apparats, 179; apparatus
merged with the state bureaucracy, 109–10, 112, 172, 182;
Bolshevik, 134; conservative
members of, 162, 163; corruption in, 119; democratization
of, 131–34, 150–51; and depoliticization, 175, 181–82;
and economic reform, 162; future of, 149–50; institutions
of, 101–2; leadership of, 158;
legitimacy of, linked with
public opinion, 125; and
meaningful public participation in politics, 131; and the
new line on economic man-
agement, 114–15, 184; origins
of, 21; politicization of, 131,
161, 162; professionals and intellectuals in, 131–32; and
public debate on national
problems, 116; and reform,
158, 160–61; reforming members of, 163; and social justice, 118–19; under Gorbachev's leadership, 114–15,
116, 117, 118, 125–26, 127–28,
130–33; under Khrushchev's
leadership, 101–2; under Stalin's leadership, 102
Passport system, 28
Patriarchal authoritarianism,
37
Peasants: communal agriculture
by, 15–16, 26; education of,
47; emancipation of, 14; internal passport system for, 28;
land redistributed to, 16;
mentality of vs. urban culture, 40 (*see also* Ruralization
of cities); "mirs" of, 16–17,
37; politicization of, 17; replaced by an urban working
class, 45–46; response to col-

Peasants (*continued*)
lectivization, 25–26; and the
tenacity of the rural spirit,
36–38; urban adaptation by,
35–40; urban migration by,
20, 22, 28, 34–38; village socialization patterns vs. urbanization by, 36–38. *See also* Kolkhoz peasants
Penal policies, 116
Perestroika, 99, 160–61, 162,
165, 183, 184; effects of, 157;
and end of one-party system,
172; opponents of, 166; and
possible unseating of Gorbachev, 173
Periodicals, and public opinion,
75–76
Personality, 64–66, 171; and literature on kolkhoz peasants,
150; needs and freedoms of,
96. *See also* Individuals
"Peter syndrome," 176, 177
Peter the Great, 13
Planning by the ministerial bureaucracy, 104–11; coordination of vertical and horizontal
links in, 104–5, 108; and "departmentalism," 104; eco-
nomic malfunctions and imbalances caused by, 104–7; on
the environment and ecology,
106–7; future trends in, 142;
and the "motivational" crisis,
104, 106–7, 110; and strategies for economic improvement, 107–10, 139, 142; on urbanization, 105–6, 108
Pluralism, 160, 161, 162
Police state, 178
Politbureau, 101, 163; on education in the social sciences and
the ideological disciplines,
115

Political leaders: and collective
political leadership, 60, 102;
corruption of, 119, 122; economic and social advantages
of, 118–19; frankness by, 114–
16; vs. the power of the state-
economy-party triad, 112–13;
and social justice, 118–19, 122
Political science, academic discipline of, 89–90
Political system: components of,
8; and the democratization of
a one-party system, 133–34,
150–51, 160–61; and political
participation, 157–58; and reform, 158; renovation of, 124–
26, 127–28, 130–31
*Political Undercurrents in Soviet
Economic Debates* (M. Lewin),
viii
Politics, 164; apathy in, 123;
"collective" leadership in, 60,
102; interdependence with
economics, culture, and society, viii–ix, 4–5, 7, 8, 61–62,
64, 69–70, 110, 112, 113, 117,
123, 130, 146; malfunctions
in, 104, 105; meaningful participation in, 123, 124, 125,
131; and response to individual autonomy and social microworlds, 68–71, 110; role of
professionals and intellectuals
in, 50
Pollution, public opinion of, 79
Post-Stalin period, 183
Power-ideology-culture triad,
113
Praktiki, 23, 178; decline of, 61;
and educational deficiencies
of political cadres, 57; historic
symbolism of, 45
Prava lichnosti, 66, 67. *See also*
Individuals

President and presidency, 159–60, 163–64, 171–72

Press. *See* Media

Privacy, 37; of the individual, 66–67

Productivity: discouraged by the worker pay system, 107; and labor morale, 93–94

Professionals, viii; effect of the revolution and civil war on, 58; and growth of the professional class, 45, 57; interaction with technicians, 50; party participation by, 131–32; political leadership by, 50; reduced by Stalinist purges, 59; rights demanded by, 64; and socioeconomic change, 55–56, 57; on solutions to urban problems, 79; and support of Gorbachev's policies, 124

Proletariat, 181

Propaganda, 71

Public debate on national problems, 116

Public opinion, 72–82; and attitudes on the law, 76–77; and civil society, 80–81; on ecology and pollution, 79; effect of the media on, 70–71; expressed in cultural life, 78–79; expressed in periodicals, 75–76; highlighted by the Gorbachev administration, 116, 117; on ideology, 27, 70–71, 115; and informal structures, 73–75; and the invisible college of scholars, 73; and party legitimacy, 125; power of, 74–75; in the workplace, 93–94

Rabfaki, 179

Rassoglasovannost, 61

Razlozhenie, and social injustice by political leaders, 118

Real politics, 152

Reform, xi; comparison of economic and political reform, 137, 167; "extensive" nature of, 176; by Gorbachev, ix–x, 116–20, 123, 126; vs. immutable Soviet institutions, 129–30; and the interconnection between economics, politics, and culture, viii–ix; by Khrushchev, viii, 1–2, 60, 74, 102–3, 129; by Kosygin, viii, 1–2, 62; new-line policies on, 116–20; of the party, 117; and public debate on national problems, 116; shortcuts in, 176; social, 162; Western attitudes toward, viii, 1–2, 103, 117

Republics, 174; Russian, 166; Ukranian, 166

Research Institute in Social Interdisciplinary Studies, 92

Restrictions on Soviet sociologists, 86–87. *See also* Soviet social sciences

Revolutionary and civil war: effect on agrarian reform, 15, 16, 17, 18; effect on the professional class, 58; and historical stages, 151, 180; viewed by Gorbachev, 124

Revolutions, counteractions to, 91–92

Rights: demanded by intellectual professionals, 64; for the freedom of movement, 64, 96, 106; and Gorbachev's social reforms, 117, 120; of individuals, 66

Rock bands, 78

Ruralization of cities, 20, 22, 34–37, 44; and integrated urban-rural development, 41; and the tenacity of peasant mentality, 36–38, 44
Rural nexus, 15. *See also* Agrarian nexus

Samizdats, 75, 147
Samookupaemost', and economic reform, 137
Scholars: on economic reform, 137; freedom of, 66, 69; "invisible college" of, 66, 69, 73; on urban problems, 79
"Scientific communism," 115
Scientific research, and social change, 49, 65–66, 88–89
"Services of social development," 93
"Settlements of urban character," 32
Siberia, 166; cities in, 33; rivers in, 74
Skilling, H. Gordon, 103
Small businesses, future of, 141
Social change: and education, 47–48, 52, 143, 147; engendered by specialists and the intelligentsia, 49, 50; Gorbachev's response to, 117, 122, 123; individual psychic health and freedom influenced by, 63–66; and intergenerational mobility, 54, 61; limited state response to, 110, 113, 130, 145, 146; linked with technoscientific research, 49–50; and the "motivational crisis," 104, 106–7, 110; and new forms of scholarship, 86; by peasant migration to cities, 35–38; and political response to indi-

vidual and group autonomy, 68–71; and the relationship with Stalinism, 24–26; and the restructuring of the national labor force, 52–56; and urban demography, 30–33; and urbanization, 32–33, 41–42, 43, 46, 113
Socialism, 165, 180
"Socialist competition," 107
"Socialist market," concept of, 2
Socialization: family influences on, 66–67; and urban migration, 36–38
Social justice: Gorbachev's policies on, 131; party policies on, 118
Social promotion, 177–78, 182
Social psychology, and morale in the workplace, 93–94
Social sciences. *See* Soviet social sciences
Society: and definitions of a social system, 5–6; disparities in, 5–6; interconnection with economics, culture, and politics, viii–ix, 4–5, 6–7, 8, 61–62, 64, 69–70, 110, 113, 117, 122, 123, 136, 146, 184; vs. the state, 7
Socioeconomic context of agrarian economic reform, 14–20; F. Braudel's theory on, 17–18
"Sociopsychological climate," 56, 93
Sotsiologicheskie Issledovaniia, 76, 88
Sovetskoe Gosudarstvo i Pravo, 76
Soviet government: congress, 161; "overloading" of, 113; relationship with the state, 7, 8, 109–10, 112–13; stability of,

9, 113; succession of leadership in, 9, 101, 114
Soviet period, 176, 177
Soviet social sciences, 85–100; on changes in the national labor force, 52–55; collaboration with Soviet politicians, 86–87, 95; on economic intensification, 92–93; on economic reform, 123; evolution of, 85, 86; and the "human capital thesis," 98; "human factor" in, 97, 99; improved research in, 87–88, 89; interdisciplinary collaboration with politics, 95, 97–98, 99; limitations and restrictions on, 86–87; new-line economic reforms supported by, 143; periodicals on, 88; and the political ascendance of Gorbachev, 85, 97; on social psychology, 93–94; statistical data for, 86; subfields of, 87, 90; and systems analysis, 90–92, 94–95; teachers of, 115; Western influences on, 87
Soviet studies, 178
Specialists: defined, 46; education of, 46–47, 49, 52; effect of the revolution and civil war on, 58; emergence of, 147; limitations on the efficacy and political leadership of, 50; relationship with technicians, 50, 107; and the restructuring of the national labor force, 52; salaries of, 119; social change engendered by, 49, 52; on solutions to urban problems, 79; women as, 48. *See also* Intelligentsia
Spontaneity, and collaboration

between social scientists and politicians, 95
Stalin, Joseph, 3, 5, 177, 179, 180, 182, 183; death of, 8, 101, 184; party power reduced by, 101; rise of, 23
Stalinism, 4, 8, 21–29, 168, 176, 178, 180; and the agrarian nexus, 21–22, 24; and bureaucratic growth, 22–23, 26; and culture, 26–27; described, 21; and despotism, 182; on grain supplies, 21; and merger of the party apparatus with the state bureaucracy, 109; political heritage of, 145; professionals and political cadres curtailed by, 59–60; relationship with social change, 24–26; resistance to ideological indoctrination during, 27; socioeconomic effects of, 101, 170
State, 6–8, 182; and agrarian reform, 13–14; building of, 24, 124; bureaucracy merged with the party apparatus, 109–10, 112; and "civil society," 7, 80–81; consolidation of the ruling apparatus of, 60; defined, 7; and economic organizations, 141; and economy relationship, 184; internal and external pressures on, 6; legitimacy of, 7; power of, 25–26, 112, 132; response to social change, 25–26, 110, 130, 145, 146; role in new economy, 165; viewed as the sole actor in history, 4–5
State-economy-party triad, 112–13
Statism, power of, 132–33

Statistics for sociological studies, 86
Stereotypes, reduction of, 116, 151
Stolypin, Piotr Arkadevich, 16
Systems analysis, 90–92, 94–95; emergence of, 90–91; and law, 91; political implications of, 91–92, 95

Tartar minorities, 96
Teachers of social sciences and ideological disciplines, 115
Technicians: interaction with professionals and intellectuals, 50; shortage of, 107
Technological research, 49
Television, and ideological change, 70
Terror: and the agrarian nexus, 21; resistance to, 28
Textile workers, sociological surveys of, 69
"Thaws" and "freezes," 1–2, 119
Theatrical groups, 78
"Think tanks," 79
Totalitarianism, 2–4
Trade unions, 7, 117; and the power of public opinion, 75
Transportation, 46
Trotsky, Leon, 180; on the state bureaucracy, 109
Tsarist Russia, 5, 181; agrarian development in, 13–17; urban housing in, 20

United States, 168
Urbanization, viii, 30–42, 175, 183; and agrarian economic reform, 20; and bureaucratic management, 175; crucial role of, in Russian/Soviet history, 28–29; and demographic change, 30–32, 145–46; and the development of capitalism, 19; and the development of an intellectual urban workforce, 44–45, 54; and the emergence of a new labor force, 43–56; and the growth of Soviet social sciences, 86; history of, 30–31, 43; individual autonomy fostered by, 63–68; and integrated urban-rural development, 41; and ministerial planning problems, 105–6, 108; in the 1960s, 31; vs. peasant mentality, 40; vs. peasant socialization, 36–38; and the ruralization of cities, 20, 22, 34–37, 44; social change catalyzed by, 32–33, 41–42, 43, 46, 158; speed of, 183; and Western perspectives on Soviet change, 33
Urlanis, V. Ts., 20
Uskorenie, 116, 162

Vedomstva: defined, 104; planning by, 104–5; power of, 109
Vedomstvennost: defined, 104; linked with economic and political malfunctions, 104–6
Verticalism in economic planning, 104–5; coordinated with horizontal structures, 108
Vestnik, 76
Village socialization vs. urbanization, 36–38
Vysotskii, Vladimor, 78

Walker, Martin, 79; on the Brezhnev administration, 2, 114
"War communism," 152

Warehouses, unsalable merchandise in, 107, 108
Waste and shortages in the Soviet economy, 107–8
Weber, Max: on the bureaucratization of socialism, 89; on capitalism and urbanization, 19
Western attitudes: on free markets and corporations, 140; influence of, on Soviet social sciences, 87; and limited perspectives on the Soviet Union, 5, 33, 103; on sexual behavior and marital relations, 68; on Soviet reform, viii, 1–2, 103, 117; and Soviet urbanization, 33; on totalitarianism, 3–4
Women: and the "cultural revolution," 48; education of, 47–48; emancipation of, 48
Workers: compared with kolkhoz peasants, 46; education of, 143; Gorbachev administration supported by, 124; increased autonomy of, 142; and the merger of the intellectual and physical labor, 51–52; morale of, 93–94; pay system of, 107; social role of, 97; in the Stalinist period, 25; and the structure of the labor force, 51
Workplace, democratization of, 132
World War I, 176, 177
World War II, 8, 48, 176

Yeltsin, Boris. *See* Eltsin, Boris

Zaslavskaia, Tatiana, on the role of sociology in Soviet politics, 86–87, 99–100
Zastoi, 166
Zatraty, 107
Zinonev, Grigory Yevseyevich, 180